The Ultimate Jordanian Cookbook

111 Dishes From Jordan To Cook Right Now

Slavka Bodic

Copyright @2021

All rights reserved. No part of this book may be reproduced in any form without writing permission in writing from the author. Reviewers may quote brief passages in reviews.

No part of this publication may be reproduced or transmitted in any form or by any means, mechanical or electronic, including photocopying or recording, or by any information storage and retrieval system, or transmitted by email without permission in writing from the publisher. While all attempts have been made to verify the information provided in this publication, neither the author nor the publisher assumes any responsibility for errors, omissions or contrary interpretations of the subject matter herein.

This book is for entertainment purposes only. The views expressed are those of the author alone and should not be taken as expert instruction or command. The reader is responsible for his or her actions. Adherence to all applicable laws and regulations, including international, federal, state and local governing professional licensing, business practices, advertising, and all other aspects of doing business in US, Canada or any other jurisdiction is the sole responsibility of the purchaser or reader.

Neither the author nor the publisher assumes any responsibility or liability whatsoever on the behalf of the purchaser or reader of these materials. Any perceived slight of any individual or organization is purely unintentional. Similarity with already published recipes is possible.

Imprint: Independently published

Please sign up for free Balkan and Mediterranean recipes:
www.balkanfood.org

Introduction

Do you wish to create tasty and savory Jordanian dishes at home to appreciate and celebrate the original Jordanian flavors? Then you've discovered the ideal book for you! This cookbook will expose you to some of Jordan's most popular recipes and feasts, which you'll definitely love, especially if you enjoy foreign foods. Whether you've visited Jordan or not, this thorough cookbook will help you to recreate its traditional cuisine at home. Jordan is known for its distinct culture, languages, and cuisine, so this book is a great way to get a taste of the country's delectable cuisine.

The Ultimate Jordanian Cookbook will introduce Jordanian cuisine and its culinary culture in a way that you may have never experienced before. It brings you a variety of Jordanian recipes in one place. The cookbook is perfect for all those who always wanted to cook Jordanian food independently, without the help of a native Jordanian. Based on this Jordanian cuisine cookbook, you can create a complete Jordanian menu of your own or try all the special Jordanian recipes on different occasions. In this cookbook, you'll find popular Jordanian meals and ones that you might not have heard of. From a variety of cakes to the luscious range of breads, warming soups, Jordanian desserts, drinks, and Jordanian salads, etc., you can explore them all. And all these recipes are designed in such a simple way that those who aren't even familiar with the Jordanian culture, food, and language can still try and cook them at home without facing much difficulty.

Jordanian culinary culture and cuisine are indeed full of wonders. There's extensive use of chickpeas, eggplants, lamb meat, fruits, and vegetables. And, if you want to add all those nutri-dense ingredients to your routine diet, then give this book a thorough read, and you'll discover all your answers right away!

Here's what you'll learn in this book:
- Facts about Jordan and Jordanian cuisine
- Jordanian breakfast recipes
- Appetizers, salads, and soups
- Main Dishes and entrees
- Jordanian desserts and drinks

Let's sample all these Jordanian recipes and recreate a complete menu to celebrate the amazing Jordanian flavors and unique aromas.

Table of Contents

INTRODUCTION 3

WHY JORDANIAN CUISINE? 9

JORDAN 11

BREAKFAST 14

    JORDANIAN MEAT PIES (SFEEHA) 15
    JORDANIAN FLAT BREAD 17
    ASREYA 19
    ZAATAR BREAD 21
    MESHTAH 23
    MIDDLE EASTERN FUL MEDAMAES 25
    GREEN SHAKSHUKA 26
    SWEET FRITTERS 27
    BAGELS WITH ZAATAR AND LABNEH 28
    SHAKSHUKA 29
    FETTEH 31
    BATATA HARA 33
    ZA'ATAR MANAQIS 34

APPETIZERS AND SNACKS 36

    MUTABAL 37
    KIBBE BALLS 38
    MUHAMMARA 40
    TOMATO AND ONION MANAKEESH 41
    CHICKPEA FALAFEL 43
    OLIVE MINI PIES 45
    GARLIC AIOLI (TOUM) 46
    HUMMUS WITH BEEF 47
    SWEET PUMPKIN HUMMUS 49
    BATATA SOUFFLÉ 51
    LABNEH BALLS 53

SALADS 54

    JORDANIAN FATTOUSH SALAD 55
    JORDANIAN CUCUMBER SALAD 57
    TABBOULEH 58
    TOMATO AND CUCUMBER SALAD WITH MINT 59

- Radish Arugula Salad 60
- Yogurt Cucumber Salad with Mint 61
- Tabouli Salad 62
- Beans Salad 63
- Chicken Shawarma Salad 64
- Jordanian Lentil Salad with Garlic And Herbs 66
- Fava Bean Salad 67
- Potato Salad 68
- Jordanian Traditional Salad 69

SOUPS 70
- Red Lentil Soup 71
- Jordanian Lentil Soup with Greens 73
- Jordanian Vegetable Soup 75
- Chicken Soup 77
- Green Lentil Soup 78
- **Lentil Chard Soup** 79
- Barley Soup 80
- Green Lentil and Spinach Soup 82
- Brown Lentil Soup 83
- Lamb Lentil Soup 85
- Harira Soup 86

MAIN DISHES 88
- Lamb Shawarma 89
- Lamb Eggplant Stew 91
- Eggplant Fetteh 93
- Lamb Rice 95
- Lamb Stew 96
- Barbecued Lamb with Garlic Sauce 97
- Middle Eastern Lamb Kofta 99
- Lamb Rice Pilaf 101
- Beef Lamb Kebabs 103
- Jordanian Spiced Chicken 104
- Shish Tawook Chicken 106
- Chicken Shawarma (Middle Eastern) 107
- Mujaddara 109
- Jordanian Chicken Fatteh 110
- Kufta Kabab 112
- Jordanian Chicken and Potatoes 113
- Chargrilled Garlic Chicken 114

- Sayadieh 115
- Jordanian Fish with Tahini Sauce 117
- Shakshuka Fish Style 119
- Jordanian Baked Fish 121
- Jordanian Spicy Fish 123
- Baba Ganouj 125
- Okra Stew 126
- Perch Fillets with Tahini Sauce 127
- Jordanian Spiced Rice and Fish 129
- Jordanian-Style Snapper 131
- Samak Mashwi 133
- Jordanian Potato Kibbe 135
- Jordanian Moussaka 137
- Jordanian Roasted Vegetables with Lentils 139
- Mint Rice 141
- Red Bulgur Pilaf 142
- Jordanian Chickpea Stew 143
- Jordanian Tofu Shish with Harissa Sauce 144
- Jordanian Rice and Lentils 146
- Jordanian Green Beans 148
- Grilled Snapper with Bulgar Salad 149
- Baked Fish with Garlic and Lemon 151

DESSERTS 152

- Jordanian Baklava 153
- Qatayef 155
- Warbat 157
- Mahalebia 159
- Jordanian Semolina Pudding 160
- Jordanian Semolina Cake Halva 161
- Halawa 163
- Sweet Dumplings 165
- Sesame Cookies 167
- Jordanian Bread Pudding 169
- Maamoul 171
- Jordanian Rice Pudding 173
- Sfouf Mini Cakes 175
- Kanafeh 176
- Caramelized Dates 177
- Sesame Pistachio Cookies 178

DRINKS 180

 Sahlab 181

 Qamar Ad-Din 182

 Tamar Hindi 183

 Shaneeneh 184

 Jallab 185

 Cardamom Coffee 186

 Jordanian Rose Drink 187

 Jordanian Lemonade 188

ONE LAST THING 197

Why Jordanian Cuisine?

Jordanian culinary culture is heavily influenced from other Middle Eastern cuisines. In fact, it's a part of a wider Levantine cuisine that existed for hundreds of years in the Arab world. It has evolved over centuries of social and political development. Jordanian cuisine employs a wide range of techniques, including baking, sautéing, and grilling, as well as stuffing vegetables (carrots, leafy greens, eggplants etc.), meats (which in Jordan refers to a blend of lamb, cattle, and occasionally goat), and chicken. Roasting or cooking meals with unique sauces is also popular in Jordanian cuisine. Jordan uses olive oil as its primary cooking oil because it's one of the world's major producers of olives.

Falafel
Falafel, crisp balls of seasoned ground chickpeas, is a popular street snack in the Levant region. Falafel balls are commonly put into warm pita bread for a quick sandwich and are popular for breakfast and even late-night snacking. Falafel is piled with bundles of fresh mint, raw onions, and tomatoes. Amman's famed Hashem Restaurant serves them as classics and then served over mounds of hot flatbread.

Kunafa
This classic delicacy is thought to have swept over the Levant under Ottoman rule — along with the thick Turkish coffee, both are beloved. The kunafa has a crisp layer of pastry threads on top of tangy cheese or

cream. Kunafa is a popular way to commemorate significant occasions, but it's also a delicious afternoon snack.

Shawarma

Slow-rotating spits of sliced lamb, chicken, or beef, another import from the former Ottoman Empire, are common in Jordan's cities and towns. The thick, fatty meat is served in warm pita pockets and then sprinkled with everything from raw onions to za'atar, a spice blend based on sesame seeds, and acidic sumac that changes depending on the chef. From the street, one shawarma joint may appear to be identical to another, yet the sandwich that homesick Jordanians crave is Shawarma Reem's iconic rendition.

Hummus with fattéh

While creamy hummus has expanded well beyond the Middle East to local grocery stores all around the world, Jordan's rich variety may come as a pleasant surprise to visitors from outside the region. Fatteh hummus is a puree of delicate chickpeas that's blended with torn-up pita bread, tahini, and pine nuts and then covered with a pale green pool of olive oil, just like the original. The version served at Hashem Restaurant in Amman is silky and creamy, and it's a delight to eat with a spoon beside a platter of tangy herbs and onions.

Jordan

Jordan is an Arab country in Southwest Asia located in the northern Arabian Peninsula's stony desert. Jordan is a young country that sits on an ancient continent that has seen numerous civilizations come and go. The Jordan River separates the region from ancient Palestine, but it played an important role in biblical history. The biblical kingdoms of Moab, Gilead, and Edom, as well as the legendary red stone city of Petra, the capital of the Nabatean kingdom and the Roman province of Arabia Petraea, are all within its borders. "It is like a fairy tale city, all pink and wonderful," British visitor Gertrude Bell said of Petra.

The capital and largest city in the country is Amman—named for the Ammonites, who made the city their capital in the 13th century BCE. Amman was later a great city of Middle Eastern antiquity, Philadelphia, of the Roman Decapolis, and now serves as one of the region's principal commercial and transportation centers as well as one of the Arab world's major cultural capitals.

Jordan, which is slightly smaller in area than Portugal, is bordered on the north by Syria, the east by Iraq, the southeast and south by Saudi Arabia, and the west by Israel and the West Bank. The West Bank (so named because it is immediately west of the Jordan River) was under Jordanian rule from 1948 to 1967, but Jordan relinquished its claim to the territory in 1988. Jordan has a coastline of 16 miles (26 kilometers) on the Gulf of Aqaba in the southwest, where Al-Aqabah, the country's only port, is located.

Jordan's climate varies from Mediterranean in the west to desert in the east and south, but the country is arid overall. The Mediterranean Sea's proximity has the greatest impact on climates, while continental air masses and height also have an impact. Average monthly temperatures in Amman, in the north, range from 46 to 78 degrees Fahrenheit (8 to 26 degrees Celsius), whereas in Al-Aqabah, in the far south, they range from 60 to 91 degrees Fahrenheit (16 to 33 degrees Celsius). The prevailing winds are westerly to southwesterly across the country, but hot, dry, dusty winds coming from the southeast off the Arabian Peninsula frequently occur, bringing the country's most unpleasant weather.

The vast majority of the population are Arabs, primarily Jordanians and Palestinians; nevertheless, there's a considerable minority of Bedouin, who were by far the largest indigenous community before the Arab-Israeli wars of 1948–49 and 1967. Despite being a minority in Jordan, Jordanians of Bedouin descent remain loyal to the Hashemite dynasty, which has dominated the country since 1923. Despite the fact that the Palestinian population is often critical of the monarchy, Jordan is the only Arab country to award Palestinian refugees citizenship on a large scale.

Jordan is a vital part of the Arab world, and hence shares a regional cultural tradition. In Jordanian culture, the family is extremely important. Despite the fact that their numbers have decreased as more people have settled and adopted urban culture, the rural Bedouin population maintains a more traditional way of life, keeping customs passed down through the centuries.

Breakfast

Jordanian Meat Pies (Sfeeha)

Preparation time: 15 minutes
Cook time: 12 minutes
Nutrition facts (per serving): 400 Cal (22g fat, 17g protein, 10g fiber)

You can give these meat-filled pies a try because they have a good and delicious combination of crispy dough stuffed with sautéed beef.

Ingredients (8 servings)
Meat filling
1 lb. 2 oz. minced lamb meat
2 small onions, diced
4 medium tomatoes, chopped
1 teaspoon salt
¼ teaspoon cinnamon powder, optional
½ teaspoon seven spice powders
Chili flakes

Dough
2 lbs. all-purpose flour
3 tablespoons sugar
2 tablespoons active dry yeast
1 tablespoon salt
¼ cup sunflower oil
2 ¼ cups whole milk

Preparation

Mix the salt, sugar, yeast, flour, oil, and milk in a suitable bowl until it makes a dough. Knead this dough for 3-5 minutes, then cover and leave for 1 hour. Meanwhile, the blend onions with the tomatoes in a blender until smooth. Transfer the tomatoes to a bowl and stir in the chili flakes, spices, salt, and minced meat. Mix well, and then strain the excess liquid. At 400 degrees F, preheat your oven. Divide the prepared dough into golf ball-sized balls and roll each ball into a ¼ inch thick circle. Divide the beef filling at the center of each circle and pinch the two opposing edges of each circle to shape the *sfeeha* In into a square boat. Place them in a greased baking sheet and bake for 12 minutes in the oven. Drizzle lemon juice on top. Serve.

Jordanian Flat Bread

Preparation time: 15 minutes
Cook time: 7 minutes
Nutrition facts (per serving): 204 Cal (4g fat, 5g protein, 1.4g fiber)

Try this Jordanian bread for breakfast, and you'll forget about the rest. The recipe is simple and gives you soft and fluffy flatbreads that you can enjoy in a number of ways.

Ingredients (8 servings)
1 ¼ cup water
2 tablespoons olive oil
½ teaspoon white sugar
1 ½ teaspoon salt
3 cups flour
1 ½ teaspoon dry active yeast

Preparation
Add the yeast, sugar, and water to a mixing bowl and mix well, and then leave for 10 minutes. Stir in oil, salt, and flour. Next, mix well until it comes together as a smooth dough. Knead this prepared dough on a lightly floured surface and divide it into 8 equal parts. Spread each dough into a ⅛-inch-thick circle. Place the flatbread in baking sheets and bake them for 5-7 minutes in the oven at 475 degrees F, until golden brown. Serve warm.

Asreya

Preparation time: 10 minutes
Cook time: 10 minutes
Nutrition facts (per serving): 216 Cal (14g fat, 4g protein, 1g fiber)

The famous Jordanian bread is here to make your breakfast special. You can always serve this bread with fresh berries smoothie.

Ingredients (6 servings)

2 lbs. 4 oz. all-purpose flour
½ teaspoon salt
⅓ cup sugar
2 cups lukewarm water
1 cup white sesame seeds
2 tablespoons instant yeast

Glaze

1 cup of water
2 tablespoons flour
2 tablespoons olive oil
A pinch of salt

Preparation

Mix the yeast with the sugar and the warm water in a bowl. Leave it for 5 minutes, add flour and salt, and then mix well until smooth. Place this prepared dough in a greased bowl, cover and leave for 1 hour. Divide the dough into 9 portions. Spread each dough portion on the working surface into ½ inch thick and 8-inch round circle. Use a 4-inch round cookie cutter to cut a hole at the center. Place the dough circles in a baking sheet lined with parchment paper. At 450 degrees F, preheat your oven. Prepare its glaze by mixing all its ingredients in a saucepan and cook until it thickens. Brush the glaze on top of the dough rounds and drizzle sesame seeds on top. Bake them for 10 minutes in the preheated oven. Allow them to cool and then serve.

Zaatar Bread

Preparation time: 15 minutes
Cook time: 20 minutes
Nutrition facts (per serving): 381 Cal (6g fat, 13g protein, 1g fiber)

If you're bored with the usual morning bread, then these Jordanian Zaatar crackers are one unique option to go for. Enjoy them with crispy bacon and eggs.

Ingredients (6 servings)
Dough
2 cups all-purpose flour
3 tablespoons olive oil
1 tablespoon sugar
⅔ cup warm water
½ teaspoon salt

Filling
½ cup zaatar
2 tablespoons sumac
⅓ cup sunflower oil
A pinch of sea salt

Preparation
At 300 degrees F, preheat your oven. Mix the flour with the oil, salt, and sugar. Stir in warm water, mix well, and knead the dough until smooth. Divide this dough into three equal portions. Mix the sumac, zaatar, oil, and sea salt in a bowl. Roll each dough piece into 2 inches squares.

Spread the zaatar filling on top and place them in a baking sheet lined with parchment paper. Bake for 20 minutes until golden brown. Serve.

Meshtah

Preparation time: 10 minutes
Cook time: 15 minutes
Nutrition facts (per serving): 368 Cal (11g fat, 12g protein, 1g fiber)

Do you want to enjoy some pancake rolls with your favorite toppings on top? These apple cinnamon rolls are quick to make and easy to serve.

Ingredients (8 servings)
Dough
2 cups all-purpose flour
¼ cup canola oil
1 tablespoon active dry yeast
2 tablespoons fine bulgur
1 cup warm full cream milk
1 teaspoon salt
1 tablespoon sugar
1 ½ tablespoon anise seeds

Glaze
1 cup of water
2 tablespoons flour
2 tablespoons olive oil
A pinch of salt
Sesame seeds, for topping

Preparation

Soak the bulgur in one cup of water for 30 minutes and then drain. Mix the flour with yeast, bulgur, anise seed, salt, and sugar in a bowl. Stir in the oil and warm milk and then mix well until smooth. Cover and leave this dough for 2 hours. Prepare the glaze by mixing all its ingredients in a saucepan and cook to a boil. Divide the prepared dough into 8 balls and roll each into 6 inches long and 1-inch-thick bread. Place each bread on a suitable baking sheet lined with parchment paper. Leave the bread for 8 minutes. At 400 degrees F, preheat your oven. Brush the glaze over the bread and drizzle sesame seeds on top. Bake the bread in the preheated oven for 10-15 minutes until the bread is golden brown. Slice and serve warm.

Middle Eastern Ful Medamaes

Preparation time: 10 minutes
Cook time: 10 minutes
Nutrition facts (per serving): 316 Cal (7g fat, 22g protein, 18g fiber)

Enjoy this fava beans Ful Medamaes meal on your Jordanian breakfast menu. Serve these beans with warm flatbread and yogurt.

Ingredients (6 servings)
1 teaspoon salt
5 garlic cloves
1 lemon, juiced
2 tablespoons tahini paste
1 (15 ½ oz.) can of chickpeas
1 teaspoon ground cumin
½ bunch parsley
1 tomato, chopped
3 (14 oz.) canned, cooked fava beans
Olive oil, for serving

Preparation
Mix the fava beans and chickpeas in suitable a cooking pot and cook for almost 10 minutes with occasional stirring. Mix and ½ of this chickpea mixture with salt, crushed garlic, lemon juice, tahini paste, and cumin. Add this mixture to the rest of the fava beans mixture and mix well. Stir in the tomatoes, parsley, and cayenne pepper. Drizzle olive oil on top and serve.

Green Shakshuka

Preparation time: 15 minutes
Cook time: 15 minutes
Nutrition facts (per serving): 410 Cal (6g fat, 10g protein, 1.4g fiber)

Try this spinach shakshuka for your breakfast, and you'll forget about the rest. The recipe is simple and gives you lots of nutrients in one place.

Ingredients (6 servings)
¼ cup of olive oil
1 medium onion, diced
1 small hot pepper, diced
5 garlic cloves, chopped
3 tablespoons coriander, diced
3 tablespoons parsley, diced
½ teaspoon salt
¼ teaspoons black pepper
12 oz. fresh spinach, chopped
1 tablespoon fresh lemon juice
6 large eggs
¼ cup of Feta cheese, crumbled

Preparation
Sauté the onion and hot pepper with oil in a pan until soft. Stir in the black pepper, salt, herbs, and garlic. Next, then cook for 3 minutes. Add lemon juice and spinach and then cover to cook on low heat for 7 minutes. Spread the mixture in the pan. Make a small well in this mixture and crack one egg into each. Cover and cook for 5 minutes. Garnish with cheese. Serve.

Sweet Fritters

Preparation time: 10 minutes
Cook time: 20 minutes
Nutrition facts (per serving): 244 Cal (10g fat, 8g protein, 2.5g fiber)

These sweet fritters are a classic Jordanian meal, great for breakfast and for side meals. You can try these fritters with cheese dip or a fruit smoothie.

Ingredients (6 servings)
2 ½ cups all-purpose flour
¼ cup canola oil
3 tablespoons sugar
2 tablespoons white sesame seeds
2 tablespoons whole anise seeds
1 tablespoon powdered milk
1 cup lukewarm water
1 ½ tablespoon active dry yeast
3 cups canola oil for deep frying

Preparation
Mix the anise seeds, sesame seeds, dry yeast, flour, sugar, milk, and oil in a bowl. Stir in lukewarm water and then mix well. Knead this dough until smooth, cover and leave this dough for 1 hour. Divide the prepared dough into 22 balls. Roll each dough piece into ½ thickness. Cut three holes at the center and leave them for 25 minutes. Add the oil to a cooking pot and heat for deep frying. Deep fry the dough in the hot oil until golden brown. Remove the fried fritters to a plate using a slotted spoon. Serve.

Bagels With Zaatar and Labneh

Preparation time: 15 minutes
Cook time: 22 minutes
Nutrition facts (per serving): 320 Cal (25g fat, 15g protein, 5.4g fiber)

It's about time to try some Jordanian bagels with zaatar and labneh on the breakfast menu and make it taste more diverse in flavors. Serve warm fresh from the oven.

Ingredients (8 servings)
3 ½ cups bread flour
1 ½ tablespoon sugar
2 teaspoons active dry yeast
1 ¼ cups lukewarm water
1 ½ teaspoon salt
1 ½ tablespoon honey, for the boiling water

Preparation
Mix the flour with salt, dry yeast, and sugar in a large ceramic bowl. Stir in the lukewarm water, and mix well until smooth. Cover and leave this dough for 2 hours. Divide the dough into 8 equal-sized balls. Shape each piece into a bagel and place them on a suitable baking sheet. Cover and refrigerate for 7 hours. At 425 degrees F, preheat your oven. Boil water in a cooking pot along with honey. Add 3 bagels to this mixture and cook for 1 minute per side. Transfer the bagels to a plate using a slotted spoon. Cook the remaining bagels in the same way. Place all the bagels on a suitable baking sheet and drizzle zaatar on top and bake for 20 minutes until golden brown. Allow bagels to cool and serve.

Shakshuka

Preparation time: 15 minutes
Cook time: 29 minutes
Nutrition facts (per serving): 306 Cal (15g fat, 7g protein, 2g fiber)

The Jordanian shakshuka is a delicious morning meal you can try every day; it's best to serve with butter on top and toasted bread on the side.

Ingredients (4 servings)

2 tablespoons olive oil
1 onion, peeled and diced
3 garlic cloves, peeled and sliced
1 chile pepper, stemmed, sliced and deseeded
1 ½ teaspoon salt
1 teaspoon black pepper
1 teaspoon paprika, smoked
1 teaspoon caraway seeds, crushed
1 teaspoon cumin seeds crushed
½ teaspoon turmeric
2 lbs. ripe tomatoes, cored and diced
2 tablespoons tomato paste
2 teaspoon honey
1 teaspoon red wine vinegar
1 cup loosely packed greens, chopped
4 oz. feta cheese, cubed
4 eggs

Preparation

Sauté the onions and the garlic with oil in a skillet for 5 minutes. Stir in the spices, black pepper, salt and chili pepper and then sauté for 1 minute. Add the vinegar, honey, tomato paste, and tomatoes and cook for 15 minutes with occasional stirring. Add the chopped greens and make six wells in the mixture. Crack one egg into each well, cover and cook for 8 minutes on low heat. Add the feta cheese to the mixture. Leave for 5 minutes and serve.

Fetteh

Preparation time: 15 minutes
Cook time: 20 minutes
Nutrition facts (per serving): 213 Cal (20g fat, 12g protein, 7g fiber)

The Jordanian chickpea fetteh breakfast is prepared with basic ingredients yet tastes so delicious. Serve it with warm buns and crispy bacon.

Ingredients (6 servings)

2 lbs. of Greek yogurt
2 loaves of pita bread
16 oz. can of chickpeas
2 tablespoons tahini
½ of a lemon
6 garlic cloves
4 tablespoons olive oil
1 tablespoon salt
1 tablespoon black pepper
1 teaspoon of cumin
1 cup of pine nuts
¼ stick of butter
1 teaspoon of baking soda
Parsley to garnish

Preparation

Cook the chickpeas with baking soda in a cooking pot to warm them up. Cut the pita bread into squares and sear in a skillet greased with cooking oil until golden brown. Mix the yogurt with garlic, black pepper, salt, lemon juice, and tahini in a bowl. Sauté the pine nuts with butter in a skillet until golden brown. Place the pita bread on the serving plate and top it with the yogurt mixture and chickpeas. Garnish with cumin and parsley. Serve.

Batata Hara

Preparation time: 10 minutes
Cook time: 20 minutes
Nutrition facts (per serving): 321 Cal (10g fat, 12g protein, 2g fiber)

As if the Jordanian menu is incomplete without this potato batata harra breakfast. Here's Jordan's special inspired morning meal to serve.

Ingredients (6 servings)
6 potatoes, peeled and cubed
4 tablespoons olive oil
Olive oil
2 bunches of cilantro, chopped
1 white onion, chopped
4 jalapenos, chopped
10 garlic cloves, minced
Salt, to taste
Black pepper, to taste
Garlic powder, to taste

Preparation
Sauté the potatoes with oil and salt in a skillet until golden brown. Sauté the onion, cilantro, jalapenos, and garlic in a skillet with 2 tablespoons of oil until golden brown. Add salt, garlic powder, and the remaining ingredients. Finally, mix well. Serve.

Za'atar Manaqis

Preparation time: 10 minutes
Cook time: 8 minutes
Nutrition facts (per serving): 243 Cal (11g fat, 15g protein, 1g fiber)

Best to serve at breakfast, this Zaatar Manaqis can function as a morning meal with eggs and crispy bacon. It's rich and loaded with calories and healthy fats.

Ingredients (4 servings)
Dough
1 cup lukewarm water
½ teaspoon sugar
2 ¼ teaspoon active dry yeast
3 cups unbleached all-purpose flour
1 teaspoon salt
2 tablespoons olive oil

Za'atar Topping
8 tablespoon Za'atar spice
½ cup Private Reserve olive oil

Serving
Fresh garden vegetables
Olives
Labneh or feta cheese

Preparation

Mix the water with yeast and sugar in a bowl and then leave for 10 minutes. Stir in the olive oil, salt, and flour and then mix evenly. Knead this dough for 10 minutes, then cover and leave for 30 minutes. Divide the dough into 8 balls. Place the balls in a baking sheet, cover, and leave for 30 minutes. Mix the zaatar spices with olive oil in a bowl. At 400 degrees F, preheat your oven. Roll each dough ball into a 5-inch disc. Press the center of each disc and add 1 tablespoon Zaatar at the center. Place them in a baking sheet and then bake for 8 minutes at 400 degrees F. Allow the Manaqis to cool and serve.

Appetizers and Snacks

Mutabal

Preparation time: 10 minutes
Cook time: 10 minutes
Nutrition facts (per serving): 211 Cal (16g fat, 6g protein, 6g fiber)

Mutabal is one of the most popular dips in Jordanian Cuisine, and it has this great taste from the grilled eggplant.

Ingredients (4 servings)
1 big eggplant, sliced
¼ cup tahini
¾ cup yogurt
3 cloves mashed garlic
1 teaspoon lemon juice
2 tablespoons olive oil
Salt, to taste

Preparation
Set up a grill on medium heat and grill the eggplants until soft. Allow the eggplants to cool, peel, and chop them. Transfer the grilled eggplant to a food processor. Add the tahini, yogurt, garlic, lemon juice, and salt. Blend well until smooth. Garnish with olive oil. Serve.

Kibbe Balls

Preparation time: 15 minutes
Cook time: 30 minutes
Nutrition facts (per serving): 451 Cal (32g fat, 18g protein, 1g fiber)

The Jordanian kibbe balls are one of the most delicious street foods that you can try at home. They're known for the bulgur mixed beef taste and the energizing combination of ingredients.

Ingredients (6 servings)
1 cup fine bulgur, soaked
1 lb. ground beef
1 cup kamoune
2 cups hot water
2 teaspoon salt
1 teaspoon kibbeh spice mix

Filling
1 lb. ground beef
1 onion, chopped
3 tablespoons canola oil
¼ cup pine nuts
1 tablespoon seven spices
1 teaspoon salt
½ teaspoon black pepper

Kamoune

1 cup fine bulgur
½ onion, chopped
¼ cup red bell pepper, chopped
½ cup mint leaves, chopped
½ teaspoon dried marjoram
1 tablespoon kibbeh spice mix
1 teaspoon salt

Preparation

Soak the bulgur in hot water in a bowl for 30 minutes. Grind the kibbeh spices in a grinder. Prepare the kamouneh by blending all its ingredients into a food processor. For the filling, sauté onion with 1 tablespoon of canola oil and peanuts in a skillet until golden brown. Stir in beef and sauté for 5 minutes until brown. Stir in black pepper and seven spices, then sauté for 3 minutes.

For the kibbeh balls, soak the bulgur in water and drain. Mix the beef with the rest kibbeh spice, salt and kammoune in a food processor. Take 2 tablespoons of the kibbeh dough and spread it into a round. Add a 1 tablespoon of filling at the center and wrap the dough around, then roll into a ball. At 350 degrees F, preheat oil in a cooking pot. Deep fry the kibbeh balls until golden brown. Transfer the balls to a plate using a slotted spoon. Serve.

Muhammara

Preparation time: 10 minutes
Nutrition facts (per serving): 357 Cal (24g fat, 12g protein, 0g fiber)

Have you ever tried Jordanian Muhammara? Well, here's a recipe to make some delicious roasted peppers and walnuts Muhammara recipe. Enjoy it with your favorite crackers or bread.

Ingredients (6 servings)
1 cup California walnuts, chopped
2 red peppers, chopped
2 garlic cloves, chopped
2 teaspoons red pepper paste
2 tablespoons pomegranate molasses
1 cup breadcrumbs
¼ cup olive oil
1 teaspoon Aleppo pepper, chopped
1 teaspoon salt
1 teaspoon cumin

Preparation
Blend the roasted red peppers with the red peppers and the rest of the ingredients in a blender. Serve.

Tomato And Onion Manakeesh

Preparation time: 10 minutes
Cook time: 12 minutes
Nutrition facts (per serving): 282 Cal (16g fat, 11g protein, 2g fiber)

Jordanian tomato and onion manakeesh offers an excellent serving, which has the baked dough with tomato and onions mixture on top.

Ingredients (8 servings)
Dough
3 cups bread flour
1½ teaspoon active dry yeast
1 tablespoon white granulated sugar
1 cup warm water
⅓ cup olive oil
1 teaspoon salt

Topping
3 tomatoes, chopped
2 onions, chopped
1 tablespoon sumac
2 teaspoons salt
2 tablespoons olive oil

Preparation
Mix ½ cup warm water with sugar and yeast in a large bowl. Leave it for 10 minutes. Stir in the rest of the dough ingredients, and then mix well. Knead this dough for 5 minutes. Cover and leave the dough for 1 hour.

Divide the dough into 12 balls and leave them for 45 minutes. Drain the chopped onions and tomatoes. Roll out each dough ball into a 6 inch round. Place the rounds on a suitable baking sheet. Mix the onions, oil, and tomatoes in a bowl and divide over the dough. At 425 degrees F, preheat your oven. Bake the manakeesh for 12 minutes in the oven until golden brown. Serve.

Chickpea Falafel

Preparation time: 10 minutes
Cook time: 20 minutes
Nutrition facts (per serving): 202 Cal (4g fat, 11g protein, 9g fiber)

Who doesn't like to have falafel? Vegetarians love to have falafel on the menu, and these Jordanian falafels are a must for every vegan menu.

Ingredients (8 servings)
2 cups dry chickpeas, soaked and drained
1 large yellow onion, diced
8 large garlic cloves
1 small bunch of parsley
1 small bunch of fresh coriander
2 teaspoons of baking soda

For frying
1 egg
½ teaspoon salt
1 teaspoon dry coriander
Oil

Preparation
In a food processor, combine the onion, cilantro, garlic, parsley, and drained chickpeas. Pulse many times until the mixture is soft and smooth. Mix in the baking soda thoroughly. Make falafel balls the size of small meatballs using this mixture. Refrigerate or freeze the falafel after placing it in a sealable container. To make the falafels, whisk

together an egg, coriander, and salt in a mixing basin. Coat the falafel balls in the egg mixture before browning them in heated oil over medium heat. Enjoy.

Olive Mini Pies

Preparation time: 15 minutes
Cook time: 25 minutes
Nutrition facts (per serving): 132 Cal (11g fat, 1.3g protein, 3g fiber)

These mini olive pies will satisfy your olive cringe in no time. They're quick to make and bake if you have biscuit dough at home.

Ingredients (4 servings)
½-lbs. pitted green olives, chopped
2 red bell peppers
1 small onion, finely chopped
2 tablespoons olive oil
½ teaspoon sumac
Chili pepper, to taste
Ground black pepper, to taste
2 ready-made biscuit dough (10 counts each)

Preparation
At 375 degrees F, preheat your oven. Deseed the quartered peppers and rub them with olive oil. Spread the peppers on a suitable baking sheet and bake for 15 minutes, then allow them to cool. Chop the roasted peppers. Sauté the onion with the olive oil in a cooking pan until soft. Stir in chopped peppers and the remaining ingredients. Mix well. Place the biscuit dough on the baking sheet and divide the filling into each. Fold the edges of the dough of the biscuits around the filling and bake for 10 minutes. Serve warm.

Garlic Aioli (Toum)

Preparation time: 15 minutes
Nutrition facts (per serving): 296 Cal (6g fat, 23g protein, 2g fiber)

Garlic Aioli is a popular Jordanian side that's enjoyed all over the country. It has a delightful mix of garlic, lemon juice, and mayonnaise.

Ingredients (4 servings)
½ cup garlic cloves
1½ cup canola oil
2 tablespoons lemon juice
1 teaspoon salt
¼ cup mayonnaise

Preparation
Blend the garlic with 1 teaspoon salt and the rest of the ingredients in a blender until smooth. Stir in ¼ cup mayonnaise and then mix well. Serve.

Hummus With Beef

Preparation time: 5 minutes
Cook time: 15 minutes
Nutrition facts (per serving): 356 Cal (22g fat, 17g protein, 0.3g fiber)

Jordanian hummus with beef makes a great serving if you're seeking a quick snack to make. Serve this hummus with delicious crackers and chips.

Ingredients (6 servings)
Hummus
2 cups chickpeas
2 tablespoons tahini paste
¼ cup lemon juice
2 small garlic cloves
2 tablespoons water
½ teaspoon salt
Olive oil, for serving

Beef
½ lb. minced ribeye
2 tablespoons olive oil
½ teaspoon salt
1 teaspoon seven spices
¼ teaspoon black pepper
3 tablespoon pine nuts

Preparation

Blend the chickpeas with tahini, lemon juice, garlic, water, and salt in a blender until smooth. Sauté the beef with the oil, salt, 7 spices, black pepper, and pine nuts in a skillet until brown. Spread the hummus on the serving plate and top it with a drizzle of olive oil. Add the sautéed beef on top. Serve.

Sweet Pumpkin Hummus

Preparation time: 15 minutes
Cook time: 10 minutes
Nutrition facts (per serving): 354 Cal (35g fat, 5g protein, 1.4g fiber)

If you haven't tried the sweet pumpkin hummus before, then here comes a simple and easy to cook recipe that you can easily prepare and cook at home in no time with minimum efforts.

Ingredients (6 servings)
1 can (15.5 oz.) of chickpeas
¾ cup pumpkin puree
1 tablespoon tahini paste
3 tablespoons maple syrup
1 tablespoon water
1½ teaspoon ground cinnamon
½ teaspoon salt

Pita chips
1 large pita bread
1 tablespoon olive oil
½ teaspoon salt
¼ teaspoon black pepper

Preparation
At 375 degrees F, preheat your oven. Layer a parchment paper with aluminum foil. Cut the pita bread into strips and toss with olive oil. Spread these strips in a baking sheet and drizzle black pepper and salt on

top. Bake for 10 minutes until golden brown. Blend the chickpeas with the rest of the ingredients in a blender. Serve the hummus with pita chips on top.

Batata Soufflé

Preparation time: 15 minutes
Cook time: 60 minutes
Nutrition facts (per serving): 275 Cal (9g fat, 21g protein, 2g fiber)

This Jordanian batata souffle is loaded with potatoes and breadcrumbs, another Jordanian-inspired delight that you should definitely try.

Ingredients (6 servings)
7 russet potatoes, peeled and diced
6 tablespoons salted butter
½ cup whole milk
1 lb. ground beef
1 onion, chopped
2 tablespoons olive oil
1 tablespoon seven spices
4 teaspoon salt
1 teaspoon black pepper
½ cup Italian breadcrumbs

Preparation
Boil the potatoes with water and salt in a cooking pot for 20 minutes and then drain. Sauté the onion with oil, ½ teaspoon black pepper, 1 teaspoon salt, and 1 tablespoon Seven spices in a skillet until soft. Stir in the beef and sauté until brown. At 375 degrees F, preheat your oven. Drain the boiled potatoes and mash them in a bowl. Stir in ½ cup milk, 4 tablespoon butter, ½ teaspoon black pepper, 1 teaspoon salt, and then mix well. Mix the breadcrumbs with 2 tablespoons of butter in a bowl.

Grease a 12x7 inches baking dish with cooking spray. Spread half of the mashed potatoes in the casserole dish and top it with beef mixture. Add the remaining potato mash and breadcrumbs on top. Bake for 30 minutes in the oven. Allow the souffle to cool. Finally, slice and serve.

Labneh Balls

Preparation time: 15 minutes
Nutrition facts (per serving): 245 Cal (10g fat, 13g protein, 2g fiber)

These simple, quick and easy labneh balls have no parallel. If you have some yogurt ready at home, then you can prepare them in no time.

Ingredients (6 servings)

2 (32oz.) containers yogurt
1 teaspoon salt
4 cups olive oil
2 tablespoons dried mint
2 tablespoons Aleppo pepper, chopped
2 tablespoons za'atar spice

Preparation

Layer a colander with cheesecloth. Add the yogurt to this cheese cloth and drizzle salt on top. Tie the cheesecloth and leave over the bowl for 2 days. Once the yogurt is strained, make 50 balls from this mixture. Roll them in the zaatar spice and drizzle Aleppo pepper, mint, and oil on top. Serve.

Salads

Jordanian Fattoush Salad

Preparation time: 10 minutes
Cook time: 10 minutes
Nutrition facts (per serving): 261 Cal (3g fat, 15g protein, 1g fiber)

The Jordanian Fattoush salad has a rich combination of ingredients that you can easily prepare at home. The salad is fairly easy to make and doesn't require much cooking.

Ingredients (4 servings)
Salad
1 large double pita bread, cut into triangles
3 tablespoons olive oil
Salt, to taste
Black pepper, to taste
1 romaine lettuce head, chopped
1 large vine-ripe tomato, diced
3 Persian cucumbers, quartered
½ green pepper, chopped
5 radishes, diced
2 green onions, chopped
¼ cup parsley, chopped

Dressing
3 tablespoons olive oil
2 tablespoons lemon juice
2 garlic cloves, pressed
1 teaspoon lemon zest, grated

1 teaspoon pomegranate molasses
½ teaspoon mint fresh, grated
½ teaspoon salt
Black pepper, to taste

Preparation

Sauté the pita with 3 tablespoons olive oil in a skillet until golden brown. Season the pita bread with black pepper and salt. Mix the rest of the ingredients in a bowl. Mix the olive oil with the rest of the dressing ingredients in a bowl. Pour into the salad and then mix well. Garnish with pita bread and serve.

Jordanian Cucumber Salad

Preparation time: 15 minutes
Nutrition facts (per serving): 309 Cal (12g fat, 17g protein, 3g fiber)

Do you want to enjoy some cucumber on the menu with a Jordanian twist? Then try this recipe and enjoy the best of all flavors in one single meal.

Ingredients (4 servings)
1 ½ cup parsley, chopped
5 tablespoons mint, chopped
1 tablespoon bulgur
1 small cucumber, finely chopped
2 tablespoons warm water
2 tablespoons lemon juice
7 tablespoons olive oil
1 teaspoon salt
1 teaspoon black pepper
1 tomato, chopped
1 piece of lettuce, chopped

Preparation
Soak the bulgur in warm water in a bowl for 30 minutes and then drain. Mix the rest of the ingredients in a salad bowl. Stir in the bulgur and mix well. Serve.

Tabbouleh

Preparation time: 10 minutes
Nutrition facts (per serving): 302 Cal (11g fat, 12g protein, 5g fiber)

The Jordanian Tabbouleh salad is enjoyed with all sorts of entrees, and it tastes great with sour cream on top. Have it on your dinner table for a tempting serving.

Ingredients (6 servings)
2 cups parsley, chopped
¼ cup fine bulgur
1 seeded tomato, diced
5 scallions, sliced
¼ cup mint, chopped
Juice of 2 lemons
4 tablespoon olive oil
½ teaspoon salt
Few grinds of black pepper
1 teaspoon crushed dried mint

Preparation
Soak the bulgur in cold water in a bowl for 15 minutes, then drain. Mix the bulgur with the rest of the ingredients in a salad bowl. Serve.

Tomato and Cucumber Salad with Mint

Preparation time: 5 minutes
Nutrition facts (per serving): 149 Cal (1g fat, 9g protein, 0.1g fiber)

This Jordanian Cucumber and Tomato salad is everyone's favorite go-to side meal. It's full of good taste. Simple and easy to make, it doesn't involve all sorts of ingredients.

Ingredients (4 servings)

5-inch cucumbers, cut into chunks
3 beefsteak tomatoes, cut into chunks
1 sweet onion, sliced
2 garlic cloves, minced
15 leaves fresh mint, chopped
2 tablespoons crushed dried mint
4 tablespoons olive oil
Juice of 2 lemons
Salt and black pepper, to taste

Preparation

Mix the onion, tomatoes, and cucumbers with the rest of the ingredients in a salad bowl. Serve.

Radish Arugula Salad

Preparation time: 10 minutes
Nutrition facts (per serving): 51 Cal (4g fat, 1g protein, 1g fiber)

This Radish Arugula Salad has a delightful mix of arugula with radishes and onion. Serve this mix with all your entrees and a drizzle of pepper on top.

Ingredients (6 servings)
3 cups baby arugula
4 radishes, sliced
3 tablespoons onion, chopped
1 lemon
2 tablespoons olive oil
Salt, black pepper, to taste
Garlic powder, to taste

Preparation
Mix the radishes with onion and the rest of the ingredients in a salad bowl. Serve.

Yogurt Cucumber Salad with Mint

Preparation time: 15 minutes
Nutrition facts (per serving): 144 Cal (17g fat, 16g protein, 1g fiber)

The refreshing cucumber salad is here to make your dinner menu a little more delicious and nourishing.

Ingredients (4 servings)
2 cups yogurt
1 garlic clove, minced
½ teaspoon salt
2 teaspoon crushed dried
2 tablespoon fresh mint, chopped
4 pickling cucumbers, sliced

Preparation
Mix the yogurt with mint, salt, and garlic in a salad bowl. Next, stir in the rest of the ingredients. Mix well and serve.

Tabouli Salad

Preparation time: 10 minutes
Nutrition facts (per serving): 176 Cal (17g fat, 7g protein, 3g fiber)

As if the Jordanian menu is incomplete without a Tabouli salad. It's made from bulgur and veggies, which add lots of nutritional value to this salad.

Ingredients (4 servings)
2 bunches fresh parsley, chopped
1 cup tomato, chopped
1 cup cucumber, peel and seed chopped
¼ cup fine Bulgur
½ cup fresh mint leaves, chopped
3 scallions, finely chopped
½ fresh lemon juice
⅓ cup olive oil
½ paprika
1 teaspoon salt
Black pepper, to taste

Preparation
Soak the bulgur wheat in a bowl filled with water. Leave it soaked for 20 minutes. Drain and transfer the bulgur to a salad bowl. Stir in all the tabouli salad ingredients. Toss well and serve.

Beans Salad

Preparation time: 10 minutes
Nutrition facts (per serving): 253 Cal (18g g fat, 29g protein, 3g fiber)

The famous salad with beans is great to serve as a healthy side meal. Try making it at home with these healthy ingredients and enjoy it.

Ingredients (4 servings)
2 (15 oz.) cans garbanzo beans, drained
1 (15 oz.) cans black beans, drained
½ cup onion, chopped
1 jalapeno, chopped
½ cup sun-dried tomatoes
1 pint grape tomatoes, cut in half
⅓ cup fresh dill, chopped
⅓ cup fresh basil, chopped
⅓ cup fresh Italian parsley, chopped
¼ cup lemon juice
⅓ cup olive oil
2 garlic cloves, pressed
3 tablespoons apple cider vinegar
Salt and black pepper, to taste
Feta cheese

Preparation
Mix the beans with onion and the rest of the ingredients in a bowl. Serve.

Chicken Shawarma Salad

Preparation time: 10 minutes
Cook time: 14 minutes
Nutrition facts (per serving): 243 Cal (13g fat, 4g protein, 0.2g fiber)

This colorful chicken shawarma salad is a Jordanian specialty, and it's usually served on all special occasions. It's prepared using a nice mix of avocado, olives, tomatoes, and lettuce.

Ingredients (4 servings)
Chicken Shawarma
2 tablespoons plain Greek yogurt
2 tablespoons olive oil
½ tablespoon tahini
2 garlic cloves, minced
¼ teaspoon ground cinnamon
¼ teaspoon ground coriander seed
¼ teaspoon ground cloves
¼ teaspoon ground cumin
¼ teaspoon ground fennel
¼ teaspoon smoked paprika
¼ teaspoon ground cardamom
¼ teaspoon cayenne pepper
½ teaspoon salt
4 boneless chicken thigh fillets

Salad

4 cup lettuce, shredded

2 tomatoes, diced

1 ripe avocado, diced

1 Jordanian cucumber, diced

½ red onion, chopped

½ cup Kalamata olives

⅓ cup crumbled feta

¼ cup fresh parsley, chopped

Garlic Yogurt Sauce

½ cup plain Greek yogurt

1 tablespoon tahini

1 garlic clove, minced

1 teaspoon lemon juice

Salt, to season

Preparation

Mix all the ingredients for shawarma in a bowl, cover, and marinate for 2 hours. Grill the chicken in a greased grill pan for 7 minutes per side. Cut the seared bread into strips. Sauté flatbreads with oil in a skillet until golden brown. Mix the rest of the ingredients in a salad bowl. Stir in the toasted bread and top it with grilled chicken. Serve.

Jordanian Lentil Salad with Garlic And Herbs

Preparation time: 10 minutes
Cook time: 30 minutes
Nutrition facts (per serving): 252 Cal (11g fat, 17g protein, 5g fiber)

The Jordanian lentil salad is one delicious way to complete your Jordanian menu; here's a recipe that you can try to have a delicious meal.

Ingredients (4 servings)
1 cup green lentils
4 tablespoons olive oil
12 garlic cloves, minced
¾ cup fresh mint, chopped
¾ cup fresh parsley, chopped
4 tablespoons lemon juice
1 ½ teaspoon ground cumin
¼ teaspoon ground allspice
Salt and black pepper, to taste

Preparation
Rinse and boil the lentils in a cooking pot with 3 cups water for 30 minutes and then drain. Mix the lentils with garlic, mint, parsley, lemon juice, cumin, allspice, black pepper, salt, and olive oil in a bowl. Serve.

Fava Bean Salad

Preparation time: 10 minutes
Nutrition facts (per serving): 311 Cal (10g fat, 14g protein, 13g fiber)

A fava beans salad is the right fit to serve with your middle eastern entrees. Here the beans are mixed with chickpeas and veggies for a wholesome flavor.

Ingredients (4 servings)
1 cup small fava beans, cooked
1 cup chickpeas, cooked
2 medium tomatoes
½ cup chopped parsley
3 cloves mashed garlic
1 chopped green onion
3 tablespoons lemon juice
2 tablespoons olive oil
½ teaspoon cumin
Salt and black pepper, to taste

Preparation
Take a suitable salad bowl and add all the ingredients. Mix and toss well. Serve.

Potato Salad

Preparation time: 15 minutes
Cook time: 13 minutes
Nutrition facts (per serving): 183 Cal (4g fat, 5g protein, 0.1g fiber)

The appetizing and savory potato salad makes a great addition to the side menu, and it looks fabulous when served at the table.

Ingredients (6 servings)
3 lbs. russet potatoes, peeled and diced
2 teaspoon salt
Juice of three large lemons
¼ cup olive oil
1 cup scallions, sliced
¼ cup fresh mint, chopped

Preparation
Boil the potatoes in water with a teaspoon of salt in a saucepan for 13 minutes and then drain. Mix the potatoes with the olive oil, lemon juice, and salt in a salad bowl. Stir in the mint and scallions. Serve.

Jordanian Traditional Salad

Preparation time: 10 minutes
Nutrition facts (per serving): 280 Cal (5g fat, 12g protein, 2g fiber)

This Jordanian traditional salad is made primarily from tomatoes, bell pepper, cucumber, green onion, and lettuce, which are then seasoned with zaatar and mint. The salad tastes terrific when served with sour cream and croutons.

Ingredients (4 servings)
3 medium tomatoes, diced
1 green bell pepper, seeded, chopped
½ of cucumber, seeded, chopped
5 green onions, chopped
¼ cup fresh parsley, chopped
1 small onion, chopped
Romaine lettuce, chopped

Dressing
¼ cup olive oil
¼ cup of lemon juice
2 garlic cloves, minced
1 teaspoon dried mint
1 teaspoon sumac or za'atar
½ teaspoon salt
Black pepper, to taste

Preparation
Prepare the za'atar dressing by mixing all its ingredients in a salad bowl. Stir in the rest of the ingredients and mix well. Serve.

Soups

Red Lentil Soup

Preparation time: 10 minutes
Cook time: 32 minutes
Nutrition facts (per serving): 327 Cal (15g fat, 10g protein, 1g fiber)

If you haven't tried the classic red lentil soup before, then here comes a simple and easy to cook recipe that you can recreate at home in no time with minimum efforts.

Ingredients (6 servings)

1 ½ cups red lentil
5 cups of water
½ cup carrots, chopped
1 celery stalk, chopped
1 medium onion, chopped
6 garlic cloves, chopped
½ tablespoon cumin powder
¼ teaspoon turmeric powder
½ teaspoon cayenne pepper
1 bay leaf
1 cube vegetable bouillon
Salt, to taste
½ tablespoon olive oil
Juice of ½ lemon
Parsley, chopped, for garnishing
Red chili flakes for garnishing

Preparation

Sauté the garlic, onion, and bay leaf with oil in a skillet until soft. Stir in the celery and carrot and cook for 2 minutes. Stir in 1 teaspoon water, salt, vegetable bouillon, and spices and then mix well. Add the lentils and water. Next, cook for 25 minutes. Discard the bay leaf from the soup and blend the rest with an immersion blender. Cook the soup for 5 minutes, then garnish with chili flakes, olive oil, lemon juice and parsley. Serve warm.

Jordanian Lentil Soup with Greens

Preparation time: 15 minutes
Cook time: 55 minutes
Nutrition facts (per serving): 381 Cal (26g fat, 14g protein, 0.6g fiber)

The Jordanian lentil soup with greens has no parallel in taste. It has a mix of lentils and spinach. Enjoy this soup with crispy bread.

Ingredients (8 servings)
1 tablespoon olive oil
1 medium onion, diced
2 medium carrots, peeled and diced
3 stalks celery diced
4 garlic cloves, minced
2 teaspoons cumin
2 teaspoons cinnamon
1 cup brown lentils uncooked
4 cups chicken broth
4 cups of water
1 lemon, juiced
Salt and black pepper, to taste
8 cups spinach

Preparation
Sauté the celery, carrots, and onions with oil in a skillet for 7 minutes. Stir in the black pepper, salt, cinnamon, cumin, and garlic. Next, sauté for 1 minute. Stir in the lentils, broth, lemon juice, and water. Then boil

the mixture, reduce its heat, and cook for 45 minutes. Add spinach and cook for 2 minutes. Stir in the lemon juice, black pepper, and salt. Serve warm.

Jordanian Vegetable Soup

Preparation time: 15 minutes
Cook time: 20 minutes
Nutrition facts (per serving): 248 Cal (8g fat, 12g protein, 1g fiber)

A perfect mix of veggies with chickpeas is all that you need to expand your Jordanian menu. Simple and easy to make, this recipe is a must to try.

Ingredients (4 servings)

1 Spanish onion, chopped
2 tablespoon olive oil
2 ½ cups carrots, chopped
¼ teaspoon ground red pepper
1 teaspoon ground coriander
4 garlic cloves, minced
1 ½ cups potatoes, chopped
1 teaspoon salt
4 cups vegetable stock
2 large tomatoes, chopped
10 artichoke hearts, cut into eighths
¾ cup canned chickpeas
¼ cup fresh parsley, chopped
2 lemons, cut into wedges

Preparation

Mix the vegetable stock, chickpea liquid, and artichoke heart brine in a bowl. Sauté the onion with olive oil for 5 minutes. Stir in the carrots, cover, and cook for 3 minutes. Add the garlic, coriander, and red pepper. Cover and cook for 3 minutes. Stir in the potatoes, 2 cups stock mixture, and salt, cover, and cook the soup to a boil. Reduce its heat and cook the potatoes until soft. Stir in the chickpeas, artichoke hearts, and tomatoes. Adjust the seasoning with salt, cover, and cook for 4 minutes. Garnish with lemon wedges and parsley. Serve warm.

Chicken Soup

Preparation time: 10 minutes
Cook time: 40 minutes
Nutrition facts (per serving): 368 Cal (21g fat, 8g protein, 1g fiber)

Serve the warming bowl of chicken soup and make your meal a little more nutritional. It has everything healthy in it, ranging from chicken to herbs, etc.

Ingredients (4 servings)
4 (2 lbs.) chicken thigh cutlets, fat trimmed
1 brown onion, halved, chopped
1 carrot, peeled, chopped
1 celery stick, trimmed, chopped
2 garlic cloves, chopped
2 tablespoons parsley stems, chopped
6 sprigs fresh thyme, leaves picked
8 cups of water
½ teaspoon whole black peppercorns
Salt flakes
¼ cup fresh parsley, chopped

Preparation
Add the chicken, peppercorns, water, thyme, parsley, garlic, celery, carrots, and onion to a saucepan, and then cook the mixture to a boil. Reduce its heat, cover and cook for 40 minutes. Discard the chicken bones, shred them, and return to the soup. Garnish with parsley and serve warm.

Green Lentil Soup

Preparation time: 5 minutes
Cook time: 60 minutes
Nutrition facts (per serving): 345 Cal (21g fat, 26g protein, 2g fiber)

This rich Jordanian Green Lentils Soup is a typical Jordanian entree, which is a must to have on a healthy menu. It has this rich mix of onion, green lentils, and tomato paste.

Ingredients (8 servings)
2 tablespoons grass-fed butter
1 medium onion, chopped
2 garlic cloves, minced
2 carrots, chopped
1 celery stalk, chopped
1 cup green lentils, soaked overnight
6 cups chicken broth
1 tablespoon tomato paste
1 teaspoon cumin
Sea salt, to taste
Black pepper, to taste
Olive oil
Lemon wedges

Preparation
Sauté the carrots, celery, garlic, and onion with olive oil in a skillet until soft. Stir in the black pepper, salt, broth, lentils, cumin, and tomato paste. Cook the lentils for 60 minutes on medium heat. Garnish with lemon juice and olive oil. Serve warm.

Lentil Chard Soup

Preparation time: 10 minutes
Cook time: 35 minutes
Nutrition facts (per serving): 117 Cal (1g fat, 5g protein, 2g fiber)

The lentil chard soup is made out of a mixture of potato, chard, and lentils. You can serve this soup with your favorite crusted bread.

Ingredients (4 servings)

¼ cup brown lentils
3 cups of filtered water
1 medium potato, diced
1 medium yellow onion, diced
1 teaspoon salt
1 teaspoon sumac
2 handfuls chard, chopped
Black pepper, to taste
1 lemon, juiced
Lemon wedges and black pepper, to serve

Preparation

Add the lentils, water, potato, chard stems, and onion to a cooking pot. Cook this mixture to a boil, reduce its heat, cover, and cook for 35 minutes. Stir in the chard leaves, black pepper, and salt. Garnish with lemon wedges. Serve warm.

Barley Soup

Preparation time: 10 minutes
Cook time: 1 hour 31 minutes
Nutrition facts (per serving): 330 Cal (29g fat, 7g protein, 3g fiber)

Try this Jordanian barley soup with your favorite herbs on top. Adding a dollop of cream or yogurt will make it even richer in taste.

Ingredients (8 servings)
2 quarts chicken stock
2 tablespoons olive oil
1 medium onion, diced
1 cup uncooked pearl barley
1 teaspoon turmeric
1 lime, juiced
¼ cup tomato paste
Salt, to taste
Black pepper, to taste
1 cup carrots, diced
½ cup sour cream
½ cup fresh parsley, chopped
8 lime wedges

Preparation
Sauté the onion with oil in a soup pot until soft. Stir in the pearl barley and sauté for 1 minute. Stir in the chicken stock, black pepper, salt, tomato paste, lime juice, and turmeric. Next, cook the mixture to a boil, reduce its heat, and cook for 1 hour on a simmer. Add the carrots and

cook for 30 minutes with occasional stirring. Mix the sour cream with ½ cup of the soup mixture in a bowl and return to the soup. Mix well and garnish with lime wedges and parsley. Serve warm.

Green Lentil and Spinach Soup

Preparation time: 10 minutes
Cook time: 37 minutes
Nutrition facts (per serving): 330 Cal (8g fat, 18g protein, 21g fiber)

Try this lentil spinach soup with your favorite herbs on top. Adding a dollop of cream or yogurt will make it even richer in taste.

Ingredients (2 servings)
1 tablespoon olive oil
1 onion, chopped
⅔ cup dry green lentils
1 ¾ cups water
1 tablespoon all-purpose flour
⅔ cup fresh spinach, chopped
3 tablespoons lemon juice
½ teaspoon salt

Preparation
Sauté the onion with olive oil in a cooking pot for 7 minutes until soft. Stir in the lentils and water and then cook the soup to a boil. Reduce its heat and cook for 25 minutes on a simmer. Transfer a ladle of this soup to a small bowl and stir in the flour. Mix well and return the slurry to the soup. Mix well and add the salt, lemon juice, and spinach. Stir and cook for 5 minutes. Serve warm.

Brown Lentil Soup

Preparation time: 10 minutes
Cook time: 41 minutes
Nutrition facts (per serving): 279 Cal (11g fat, 12g protein, 6g fiber)

Make this brown lentil spinach in no time and enjoy it with some garnish on top. Adding a dollop of yogurt or labneh makes it even richer in taste.

Ingredients (4 servings)

10 ½ oz. (300 g) brown lentils, soaked and rinsed
3 medium onions, sliced
3 tablespoons olive oil
4 garlic cloves, sliced
3 heaped teaspoon cumin seeds, toasted and ground
1 large bunch fresh coriander, chopped
1 ¾ liters cold water
4 tablespoons Greek yogurt
½ garlic clove, crushed
Salt, to taste
Juice of ½ a lemon
Chili flakes, to serve

Preparation

Sauté the onion with olive oil in a cooking pot for 10 minutes until soft. Stir the garlic and the cumin seeds and then sauté for 30 seconds. Add the lentils and the water and cook the soup to a boil. Reduce its heat and cook for 30 minutes on a simmer with occasional stirring. Mix the yogurt with crushed garlic, salt, lemon juice, and chili flakes in a small bowl. Serve the brown lentil soup with a dollop of this season yogurt on top. Enjoy.

Lamb Lentil Soup

Preparation time: 15 minutes
Cook time: 1 hour 55 minutes
Nutrition facts (per serving): 455 Cal (9g fat, 39g protein, 2g fiber)

Loaded with lots of calories, lamb Lentil soup is a Jordanian lamb lentils entrée that makes an amazing serving for all your meals. Enjoy it warm with your favorite bread.

Ingredients (8 servings)
2 cups parsley, chopped
1 cup mint, chopped
1 beet, peeled and chopped
1 cup red lentils
1 cup of rice
1 lb. lamb shanks
4 cups pomegranate juice
⅔ cups pomegranate molasses
⅓ cup sugar
2 tablespoons angelica seeds

Preparation
Sauté the onions with oil in a skillet until caramelized. Stir in the turmeric, garlic, and meat and then sauté for 5 minutes. Add 2 quarts of water and cook the meat on a simmer for 1 hour until the meat is tender. Stir in the lentils and the rice and then cook for 25 minutes. Add the pomegranate juice and the herbs. Then cook for another 25 minutes. Garnish with pomegranate arils, herbs, and sliced onions. Serve warm.

Harira Soup

Preparation time: 10 minutes
Cook time: 28 minutes
Nutrition facts (per serving): 141 Cal (6g fat, 4.7g protein, 1.2g fiber)

Try this super tasty Jordanian Harira soup prepared with lamb, onion, lots of seasoning, etc. Serve it to your family and to make your meals special, and you'll never stop having it; that's how heavenly the combination tastes.

Ingredients (8 servings)
Soup
7 oz. boneless lamb diced
1 oz. corn oil
5 oz. onion, small diced
3 ½ oz. ginger, minced
3 ½ oz. tomato pronto
8 cups water
3 tablespoons chicken bouillon powder
3 ½ oz. spaghetti pasta
⅔ oz. tomato paste
⅔ oz. turmeric powder
⅔ oz. cumin powder
⅓ oz. lime seasoning powder
3 ½ oz. lentil green, boiled, drained

Garnish
Lime seasoning powder
2 ½ tablespoons coriander leaves

Preparation

Sauté the onion and ginger with oil in a saucepan for 3 minutes. Stir in the lamb cubes and sauté until brown. Stir in the water, chicken bouillon powder, water, tomato paste, and Tomato pronto. Boil this mixture then Reduce its heat and cook for 10 minutes. Stir in the cumin, turmeric, chickpeas and lentils. Next, cook for 10 minutes with occasional stirring. Mix the lime seasoning with water in a bowl. Pour into the soup and garnish with coriander. Serve warm.

Main Dishes

Lamb Shawarma

Preparation time: 10 minutes
Cook time: 3 hours 30 minutes
Nutrition facts (per serving): 272 Cal (16g fat, 22g protein, 1g fiber)

If you haven't tried the Jordanian lamb shawarma before, then here comes a simple and easy to cook recipe that you can recreate at home in no time with minimum effort.

Ingredients (8 servings)
4 lbs. lamb shoulder (bone-in)

Shawarma Paste
3 garlic cloves, minced
1 tablespoon ground coriander
1 tablespoon ground cumin
1 tablespoon ground cardamom
1 teaspoon cayenne pepper
2 teaspoons smoked paprika
1 ½ teaspoon salt
½ teaspoon black pepper
¼ cup olive oil
3 tablespoons lemon juice
2 cups of water

Preparation
At 350 degrees F, preheat your oven. Mix all the paste ingredients in a bowl. Rub this paste over the lamb liberally. Place the prepared lamb in

a roasting pan, cover and marinate for 24 hours. Pour a little water around the lamb, cover with the foil, and roast for 3 hours in the oven. Remove the foil, brush it with cooking juices, and bake for 30 minutes. Serve warm.

Lamb Eggplant Stew

Preparation time: 15 minutes
Cook time: 8 hours 30 minutes
Nutrition facts (per serving): 363 Cal (10g fat, 29g protein, 0g fiber)

This Jordanian lamb stew with eggplant is a healthy entrée that can be served with some coleslaw on the side, which will enhance its flavor and will make it more nutritious.

Ingredients (4 servings)
1 large eggplant, cut into cubes
6 tablespoons olive oil
1 lb. lamb, boneless and cubed
1 large onion, diced
3 garlic cloves, minced
½ cup red wine
3 tablespoon tomato paste
14 oz. canned tomatoes, chopped
2 cups lamb stock
1 bay leaf
2 teaspoons black pepper
1 teaspoon thyme
1 teaspoon ground cinnamon
½ teaspoon allspice, ground
½ teaspoon nutmeg, grated
1 teaspoon salt
Parsley to finish, chopped

Preparation

At 400 degrees F, preheat your oven. Toss the eggplant cubes with 2 tablespoons olive oil in a baking sheet and roast for 20 minutes. Sauté lamb with 2 tablespoons olive oil in a skillet until brown. Stir in the garlic and the onions then sauté for 2 minutes. Transfer all the ingredients to a slow cooker, cover the lid, and cook for 8 hours on low heat. Garnish with parsley and serve warm.

Eggplant Fetteh

Preparation time: 10 minutes
Cook time: 50 minutes
Nutrition facts (per serving): 324 Cal (16g fat, 9g protein, 14g fiber)

Let's make quick eggplant Fetteh with these simple ingredients. Mix them together and then cook to achieve great flavors.

Ingredients (6 servings)

4 eggplants, peeled and sliced
4 oz. (120 ml) olive oil
1 ½ (100 g) thin pitas, fresh
2 garlic cloves, finely sliced
1 teaspoon Aleppo chili flakes
10 oz. (300 g) natural yogurt
2 teaspoon lemon juice
2 tomatoes, grated
2 tablespoons mint leaves, torn
Black pepper, to taste
Salt, to taste
Pomegranate seeds, to garnish

Preparation

At 428 degrees F, preheat your oven. Spread all the eggplant slices in a baking tray lined with parchment paper in a single layer. Drizzle 4 tablespoons oil, salt, and black pepper over the slices and roast them for 30 minutes in the oven until brown and soft. Allow the slices to cool and switch the oven heat to 350 degrees F. Split the pit into two parts and roll each half. Slice these rolls into ⅙ inch wide strips. Toss the strips with 2 tablespoons of oil, black pepper, and ⅛th salt in a bowl. Spread these strips in a baking tray and bake for 10 minutes until golden brown. Add 2 tablespoon oil to a small saucepan and place it over medium-high heat. Stir in the chili flakes and garlic and then sauté for 3 minutes. Transfer to a bowl. Add yogurt and cook for 5 minutes. Stir in the lemon juice, eggplant, ¼ teaspoon salt, and 4 tablespoons water and cook for 5 minutes with occasional stirring. Transfer the prepared eggplant mixture to a serving bowl. Top it with mint and tomato. Garnish with toasted pita, pomegranate seeds, and garlic oil. Serve.

Lamb Rice

Preparation time: 15 minutes
Cook time: 31 minutes
Nutrition facts (per serving): 351 Cal (16g fat, 45g protein, 18g fiber)

Have you tried Jordanian lamb rice before? Well, here's a Jordanian delight that can add lamb meat and rice to your dinner table in a delicious way.

Ingredients (4 servings)
1 tablespoon ghee
1 lb. ground lamb
½ teaspoon salt
½ teaspoon black pepper
1 cup dry basmati rice
2 cups bone broth
¼ cup raw shelled pistachios
1 tablespoon fresh mint leaves, chopped
1 cup yogurt
Fresh cucumber slices, for serving

Preparation
Sauté the lamb with ghee in a skillet for 10 minutes until brown. Stir in the rice and sauté for 1 minute. Stir in the stock, cover, and cook for 20 minutes on low heat. Garnish with mint and pistachios. Garnish with yogurt and cucumber slices. Serve.

Lamb Stew

Preparation time: 10 minutes
Cook time: 25 minutes
Nutrition facts (per serving): 271 Cal (9g fat, 23g protein, 6g fiber)

Here's a simple Jordanian lamb stew recipe that's made with some basic ingredients. Serve this with some warm bread or rice.

Ingredients (4 servings)
1 lb. lamb cubes
1 onion chopped
1 potato cut into cubes
3 garlic cloves minced
¼ cup tomato paste
Salt, to taste
2 cups hot water
3 whole cardamoms
¼ teaspoon cinnamon powder
3 whole cloves
½ teaspoon cumin
1 ½ tablespoon Yamani spice mix
Oil

Preparation
Sauté the onion with oil in a pressure cooker until soft. Stir in the lamb and sauté until brown. Add garlic and spices then sauté for 1 minute. Add water and tomato paste then cook the mixture to boil. Add the potatoes, cover with the pressure-cooking lid, and cook for 15 minutes on low heat. Once done, release the pressure completely and then remove the lid. Mix well and serve warm.

Barbecued Lamb with Garlic Sauce

Preparation time: 10 minutes
Cook time: 60 minutes
Nutrition facts (per serving): 456 Cal (33g fat, 41g protein, 2g fiber)

This barbecued lamb with garlic sauce is known as the classic Jordanian dinner. The lamb shoulder with thick garlic sauce on top tastes heavenly with rice and bread.

Ingredients (4 servings)

2 ½ lbs. boned lamb shoulder
2 teaspoons allspice
⅓ cup olive oil
1 baby cos lettuce heart, trimmed, leaves separated
14 oz. tomato medley mix halved
1 Jordanian cucumber, halved, sliced
½ small red onion, sliced
½ cup torn fresh mint leaves
¼ cup lemon juice
6 garlic cloves, peeled, chopped
1 teaspoon sea salt
¼ cup lemon juice
1 egg white
1 cup rice bran oil
2 tablespoons iced water
Jordanian bread, warmed, to serve
Jordanian garlic sauce

Preparation

Mix the lamb with ¼ cup oil and allspice in a ceramic dish. Cover and refrigerate the meat for 2 hours. Mix the garlic with lemon juice and salt in a food processor. Add the egg white and mix well. Pour in the oil and continue blending. Slowly pour in the iced water and continue mixing fluffy. Transfer the mixture to a bowl, cover, and refrigerate. Set a barbecue grill over medium-low heat and grill the lamb for 15 minutes. Flip and cover the lamb for 35 minutes. Transfer the lamb to a plate, cover and leave for 10 minutes. Mix onion, mint, cucumber, tomato and lettuce in a bowl. Stir in the remaining oil, lemon juice, black pepper, and salt. Slice the cooked lamb and serve with garlic sauce and salad.

Middle Eastern Lamb Kofta

Preparation time: 10 minutes
Cook time: 14 minutes
Nutrition facts (per serving): 515 Cal (27g fat, 29g protein, 1.2g fiber)

Eastern Lamb Kofta provides another popular entrée that's known for rich meaty flavor. Serve them with toasted burgers and salad.

Ingredients (8 servings)
¼ cup pine nuts
¼ cup almonds
¼ cup walnuts
1 small yellow onion, chopped
3 garlic cloves, chopped
1 small red bell pepper, chopped
1 small jalapeño pepper, chopped
½ cup cilantro leaves
2 lbs. ground lamb
¾ teaspoon ground cumin
¼ teaspoon ground cinnamon
¼ teaspoon ground cardamom
¼ teaspoon ground cloves
1 ½ teaspoon salt
¼ teaspoon white pepper
Tzatziki and hummus, for serving

Preparation

Blend the nuts in a food processor until chopped. Roast the nuts in a dry skillet over medium heat for 6 minutes. Transfer them to a bowl and stir in the rest of the ingredients. Mix this mixture in a food processor. Make 2 inch round and ½ inch thick patties out of this mixture and place them in a greased baking sheet. Cover and refrigerate them until set. Grease a grill and preheat at medium-high heat. Grill the patties for 4 minutes per side. Serve warm with hummus and tzatziki. Enjoy.

Lamb Rice Pilaf

Preparation time: 15 minutes
Cook time: 2 hours 58 minutes
Nutrition facts (per serving): 386 Cal (15g fat, 31g protein, 1g fiber)

If you haven't tried the famous lamb shoulder with sausages, apricots and lentils before, then here comes a simple and easy to cook recipe that you can recreate at home in no time with minimum effort.

Ingredients (8 servings)
4 tablespoons olive oil
2 lbs. lamb shoulder, diced
10 ½ oz. merguez sausages, chopped
2 red onions, sliced
3 garlic cloves, chopped
2 carrots, sliced
½ teaspoon ground cinnamon
½ teaspoon paprika
1 teaspoon ground cumin
½ teaspoon cumin seeds
1 teaspoon ground turmeric
4 ½ oz. dried apricots halved
4 cups chicken stock
10 ½ oz. long-grain white rice
1 ⅔ oz. dried lentils, rinsed
1 handful of parsley, chopped

Preparation

At 325 degrees F, preheat your oven. Sear the lamb meat in a skillet with ½ of the oil for 4 minutes per side until brown. Transfer the brown meat to a plate. Stir in remaining oil, carrots, garlic and onions, then sauté for 5 minutes. Add spices and mix well. Return the lamb and add the stock, seasoning, and apricots. Cover and cook for 2 hours in the oven. Add the sausages, lentils, and rice, cover, and cook for 45 minutes in the oven. Garnish with parsley and serve warm.

Beef Lamb Kebabs

Preparation time: 15 minutes
Cook time: 20 minutes
Nutrition facts (per serving): 241 Cal (11g fat, 33g protein, 0g fiber)

The beef lamb kebab with tabouli and hummus is an entrée that you must serve on the festive celebration. This recipe will add a lot of appeal and color to your dinner table.

Ingredients (8 servings)
1 lb. (500 g) minced beef
1 lb. (500 g) minced lamb
½ bunch spring onions, finely chopped
1 large handful parsley, chopped
3 teaspoons salt flakes
1 teaspoon freshly ground white pepper
1 tablespoon Baharat spices
1 teaspoon Aleppo pepper flakes
2 tablespoons olive oil
Hummus and tabouli, to serve

Preparation
Mix the beef, lamb, spring onions, parsley, white pepper, salt, Aleppo pepper flakes, and Baharat in a mixing bowl. Take a handful of this mixture and wrap it around a skewer like a sausage with a greased hand. Repeat the same steps with the remaining meat mixture. Preheat the grill on medium heat and grill the skewers for 3-4 minutes per side until brown. Serve warm.

Jordanian Spiced Chicken

Preparation time: 15 minutes
Cook time: 50 minutes
Nutrition facts (per serving): 236 Cal (17g fat, 29 protein, 2g fiber)

This quick and easy chicken with 7 spices recipe is also quite famous in the region; in fact, it's vital to try because of its nutritional content.

Ingredients (4 servings)
2 lbs. chicken, bone-in thighs
2 tablespoons olive oil
2 ½ teaspoons salt
2 teaspoons black pepper
2 tablespoons Jordanian 7-spices
1 red onion, sliced
4 garlic cloves, chopped
1 tablespoon preserved lemon, chopped
1 lemon, sliced
¼ cup Marcona almonds, slivered
Parsley, for garnish

Seven Spice
1 teaspoon cumin
1 teaspoon allspice
1 teaspoon cinnamon
1 teaspoon coriander
½ teaspoon ground cloves
½ teaspoon nutmeg
¼ teaspoon cardamom

Preparation

At 400 degrees F, preheat your oven. Mix the chicken with 7 spice, salt, and olive oil in a bowl. Add the lemon slices, preserved lemon, garlic, and onion and then mix well. Layer a baking sheet with parchment paper. Add the meat to the baking sheet and bake for 45 minutes, and then broil for 5 minutes. Toast the almonds with olive oil in a skillet until golden brown. Garnish the meat with the almonds. Drizzle with black pepper and salt. Serve warm.

Shish Tawook Chicken

Preparation time: 10 minutes
Cook time: 7 minutes
Nutrition facts (per serving): 388 Cal (11g fat, 28g protein, 3g fiber)

This Jordanian shisk tawook chicken is everything you must be looking for to make you dinner loaded with nutrients. The combination of chicken with spices makes a complete package with a mixed greens salad.

Ingredients (2 servings)
20 oz. boneless chicken breasts, cubed
1 juice and zest of lemon
2 garlic cloves, grated
1 teaspoon salt
½ teaspoon black pepper
1 tablespoon olive oil
Fresh parsley, to serve

Preparation
Mix the chicken cubes with black pepper, salt, garlic, zest, and lemon juice in a bowl. Cover and marinate the chicken in the refrigerator for 20 minutes. Add the oil to a suitable skillet and heat over medium-high heat. Sauté the chicken in the skillet for 7 minutes. Garnish with parsley and serve warm.

Chicken Shawarma (Middle Eastern)

Preparation time: 15 minutes
Cook time: 10 minutes
Nutrition facts (per serving): 519 Cal (12g fat, 20g protein, 2g fiber)

This Jordanian chicken shawarma is loved by all, young and adult. It's simple and quick to make. This delight is great to serve at dinner tables.

Ingredients (4 servings)
2 lbs. chicken thigh fillets, boneless

Marinade
1 garlic clove, minced
1 tablespoon ground coriander
1 tablespoon ground cumin
1 tablespoon ground cardamom
1 teaspoon ground cayenne pepper
2 teaspoons smoked paprika
2 teaspoons salt
Black pepper, to taste
2 tablespoons lemon juice
3 tablespoons olive oil

Yogurt Sauce
1 cup Greek yogurt
1 garlic clove, crushed
1 teaspoon cumin

A squeeze of lemon juice
Salt and black pepper, to taste
6 Jordanian pita breads, for serving
Sliced lettuce
Tomato slices

Preparation

Mix the chicken with all the marinade ingredients in a bowl. Cover and marinate the chicken in the refrigerator for 24 hours. Set a grill over medium-high heat. Grease the grilling grate with cooking spray. Grill the marinated chicken for 5 minutes per side. Allow the chicken to cool. Cut the chicken into thin slices. Mix all the yogurt ingredients in a bowl. Place the flatbreads on the working surface and divide the yogurt sauce on top. Add the vegetables and the chicken on top. Roll the flatbread and serve.

Mujaddara

Preparation time: 15 minutes
Cook time: 21 minutes
Nutrition facts (per serving): 273 Cal (13g fat, 8g protein, 2g fiber)

This lentil and rice mix taste amazing, and it simple and easy to cook. It's perfect for all the rice lovers who want to enjoy it with some lentils.

Ingredients (4 servings)
2 cups white rice
½ cup boiled brown lentils
2 onions, chopped
¼ cup vegetable oil
3 cups hot water
2 cubes of chicken stock
1 pinch salt

Preparation
Add the vegetable oil, lentils, and rice to a saucepan then stir cook for 1 minute. Pour in 3 cups water, chicken stock, and salt, cover, and cook for 20 minutes on low heat. Meanwhile, sauté the onion with oil in a separate pan until golden brown. Add the onions on top of the rice and serve warm.

Jordanian Chicken Fatteh

Preparation time: 15 minutes
Cook time: 32 minutes
Nutrition facts (per serving): 722 Cal (57g fat, 36g protein, 4g fiber)

The famous Jordanian chicken fatteh is a must on the Jordanian menu. Try cooking it at home with these healthy ingredients and enjoy.

Ingredients (4 servings)
4 bone-in chicken breasts
Salt, to taste
1 tablespoon apple cider vinegar
2 dried bay leaves
2 cinnamon sticks
4 whole cardamom pods, crushed
6 cloves
Water
Olive oil
1 medium yellow onion, peeled and sliced
3 garlic cloves, crushed
1 teaspoon sweet Spanish paprika
1 teaspoon ground sumac
½ cup toasted pine nuts
½ cup toasted almonds, sliced
Parsley leaves, for garnish
2 loaves Jordanian pita bread, toasted and broken into chips

Mint Yogurt Sauce

1 ½ cup yogurt

2 garlic cloves, crushed

½ cup fresh mint, chopped

1 pinch salt

Preparation

Mix all the ingredients for the mint yogurt sauce in a bowl. Cover and refrigerate this sauce. Add the chicken enough water to cover, cinnamon sticks, cardamom, bay leaves, salt, and apple cider vinegar. Cover and cook for 20 minutes and then drain. Cut the chicken into cubes. Sauté the onions with oil in a skillet for 4 minutes. Stir in the garlic and sauté for 30 seconds. Add the chicken, sumac, and paprika. Next, sauté for 7 minutes. Stir in the toasted nuts and garnish with parsley leaves. Serve the chicken on top of the pita bread and garnish with yogurt sauce.

Kufta Kabab

Preparation time: 15 minutes
Cook time: 15 minutes
Nutrition facts (per serving): 236 Cal (13.8g fat, 18g protein, 1.7g fiber)

A perfect mix of lamb meat with spices and herbs, these kebabs taste heavenly when grilled in the grill.

Ingredients (4 servings)
1-lb. (500 g) ground lamb
2 cloves garlic, mashed
1 cup parsley, chopped
½ teaspoon paprika
¼ teaspoon black pepper
1 teaspoon salt
Oil, for grilling
12 metal skewers

Preparation
Mix the minced lamb with the garlic, parsley, paprika, black pepper, and salt in a mixing bowl. Make about 12 balls from this mixture and press the meatballs around a skewer to make a sausage. Preheat a grill over medium heat and grease its grilling grates. Grill each skewer for 5 minutes per side. Serve warm.

Jordanian Chicken and Potatoes

Preparation time: 15 minutes
Cook time: 48 minutes
Nutrition facts (per serving): 337 Cal (18g fat, 28g protein, 2g fiber)

If you haven't tried the famous Jordanian chicken and potatoes before, then here comes a simple and easy to cook recipe that you can recreate at home in no time with minimum efforts.

Ingredients (4 servings)
2 tablespoons olive oil
3 potatoes, sliced
4 lemons, juiced
10 garlic cloves, crushed
1 chicken bouillon cube, mixed with ½ cup hot water
¼ cup olive oil
1 teaspoon seven spice powder
½ teaspoon salt
¼ teaspoon black pepper
6 chicken breasts, sliced
8 garlic cloves, whole and peeled

Preparation
At 390 degrees F, preheat your oven. Sauté the potatoes with oil in a large skillet for 4 minutes per side. Mix the lemon juice, black pepper, salt, seven spice, olive oil, water, stock cubes, and garlic in a bowl. Place the chicken in a baking dish and pour half of the sauce over the mixture. Add the garlic cloves and the potato slices around the chicken. Pour remaining sauce on top, cover with a foil, and bake for 30 minutes in the oven. Flip the chicken and bake for 10 minutes. Serve warm.

Chargrilled Garlic Chicken

Preparation time: 15 minutes
Cook time: 35 minutes
Nutrition facts (per serving): 338 Cal (9g fat, 28g protein, 0g fiber)

The chicken tastes great when seasoned with special sumac marinade. Adding the special Jordanian garlic sauce to the chicken makes it soft, moist, and juicy.

Ingredients (6 servings)
1 whole chicken, butterflied
¼ cup toum (Jordanian garlic sauce)

Marinade
½ teaspoon cayenne pepper
1½ teaspoon paprika
1 teaspoon ground cumin
1 tablespoon sumac
⅛ teaspoon ground cinnamon
6 garlic cloves, crushed
⅓ cup lemon juice
⅓ cup olive oil

Preparation
Mix the chicken marinade in a bowl. Rub this marinade over the chicken and place it on a suitable baking sheet. Cover and refrigerate overnight. At 400 degrees f, preheat your oven. Roast the chicken for 25 minutes. Flip the chicken after every 10 minutes. Cut into pieces and serve warm with bread, pickles, and toum.

Sayadieh

Preparation time: 5 minutes
Cook time: 45 minutes
Nutrition facts (per serving): 424 Cal (21g fat, 21g protein, 1g fiber)

The Jordanian Sayadieh is loved by all due to its amazing blend of onion, rice and fish cod. This meal makes an irresistible serving for the table.

Ingredients (4 servings)
Onions and the rice
3 tablespoons olive oil
4 onions, sliced
1 teaspoon cumin powder
½ teaspoon turmeric powder
½ teaspoon cinnamon powder
1 ½ teaspoon salt
½ teaspoon black pepper powder
4 cups of water
1 tablespoon tomato paste
2 cups basmati rice, soaked

Fish
2 tablespoons olive oil
1 ½ lbs. white fish cod, cut into pieces
1 teaspoon cumin powder
½ teaspoon paprika powder
1 pinch each salt and black pepper

Garnish

Toasted pine nuts or almond slivers
Fresh parsley, chopped

Preparation

Sauté the onion with oil in a large pot over medium-high heat for 15 minutes. Blend the onions with cumin, 1 cup water, turmeric, black pepper, salt, cinnamon, and tomato paste in a blender until smooth. Pour this sauce into a saucepan and add the remaining 3 cups of water and rice. Boil this mixture, cover, and cook for 20 minutes on low heat. Sear the fish in a skillet, greased with cooking oil. Drizzle the spices over the fish and cook for 5 minutes per side. Add fish to the rice and garnish with the parsley, nuts, and caramelized onion. Serve warm.

Jordanian Fish with Tahini Sauce

Preparation time: 15 minutes
Cook time: 30 minutes
Nutrition facts (per serving): 261 Cal (22g fat, 14 protein, 2g fiber)

This Jordanian fish with tahini sauce is a must to have on this Jordanian menu. It has an easy mix of rice, tahini sauce, and fish.

Ingredients (4 servings)
Tahini sauce and the rice
1 garlic cloves, minced
1 bunch flat-leaf parsley
¾ cup tahini
⅓ cup lemon juice
¾ water
1 pinch salt
1 cup basmati rice
4 tablespoons unsalted butter
2 tablespoons olive oil
1 yellow onion, peeled and sliced
½ cup pine nuts

Fish and the assembly
2 lbs. fish filet
2 tablespoons olive oil
1 pinch salt and black pepper
2 tablespoons butter
2 limes, quartered
½ bunch cilantro, chopped

Preparation

Blend the garlic with the parsley in a food processor. Next, add tahini and blend. Stir in the lemon juice, a pinch of salt, a drizzle of water and then mix well. Sauté the onion with butter, oil, and a pinch of salt in a skillet until brown. Transfer the onion to a plate. Stir in the pine nuts and sauté until golden brown. Boil the water with the salt in a cooking pot and stir in the rice. Cook 10 minutes and then drain. Rub the fish with olive oil, black pepper, and salt. Sear the fish in the greased skillet for 5 minutes per side. Mix rice with 2 tablespoon butter, pine nuts, and onions in a bowl. Spread the rice on a serving platter. Place the fish on top of the rice. Garnish with pine nuts and lime slices. Serve warm.

Shakshuka Fish Style

Preparation time: 15 minutes
Cook time: 29 minutes
Nutrition facts (per serving): 493 Cal (15g fat, 30g protein, 1.7g fiber)

A perfect mix of fish fillets with the delicious shakshuka base is a must to try. Serve warm with your favorite side salad for the best taste.

Ingredients (4 servings)
Fish Fillet
2 teaspoons ground coriander
2 teaspoons sumac
1 ½ teaspoon ground cumin
1 teaspoon dill weed
1 teaspoon turmeric
1 large, sweet onion, chopped
Olive oil
8 garlic cloves, chopped
1 jalapeno peppers, chopped
5 medium ripe tomatoes, diced or chopped
3 tablespoons tomato paste
1 lime, juice
½ cup water
Salt and black pepper, to taste
2 lbs. cod fillet, cut into pieces
½ cup fresh parsley, chopped
1 tablespoon fresh mint leaves, chopped

Preparation

Mix the turmeric with the dill, cumin, sumac, and coriander in a bowl. Sauté the onions with 2 tablespoons of oil in a skillet for 2 minutes. Stir in the jalapeno and garlic, then sauté for 2 minutes. Stir in the tomatoes and ½ of the spice mixture. Stir in the black pepper, salt, water, lime juice, and tomato paste. Mix well, cover, and cook for 10 minutes with occasional stirring. Place the fish in the tomato mixture, cover, and cook for 15 minutes. Garnish with mint leaves and parsley. Serve warm.

Jordanian Baked Fish

Preparation time: 15 minutes
Cook time: 47 minutes
Nutrition facts (per serving): 357 Cal (10g fat, 13g protein, 2g fiber)

The Jordanian baked sea bream fish with tahini sauce is famous for its unique taste and aroma, and now you can bring those exotic flavors home by using this recipe.

Ingredients (8 servings)
4 lbs. sea bream fish

Tatbileh filling
2 green chilis, chopped
5 garlic cloves, crushed
¼ cup lemon juice
Slices of 2 lemons
1 tablespoon lemon rind
1 tablespoon cumin
1 tablespoon olive oil
Salt and black pepper, to taste

Rub
¼ cup cooking oil
1 teaspoon coriander
1 teaspoon cayenne pepper
Salt and black pepper, to taste

Tahini sauce
1 medium onion, chopped
2 tablespoons cooking oil
10 garlic cloves, crushed
2 tablespoons coriander powder
1 cup tahini
2 cups water
1 cup lemon juice
½ cup walnuts, chopped
Salt and black pepper, to taste
Red chili flakes, crushed
Garnish with fried almonds, red chili chopped, pine nuts, chopped coriander

Preparation
Mix all the rub ingredients in a bowl and rub over the fish liberally. Mix all the filling ingredients in a bowl. Stuff the fish with the prepared filling and cover to marinate for 15 minutes. Cover the fish with a foil sheet and bake for 20 minutes. Sauté the onions with 2 tablespoons of oil in a skillet until soft. Stir in the garlic and sauté for 2 minutes. Add the walnuts, red chili flakes, black pepper, salt, tahini sauce, and coriander. Next, cook for 10 minutes. Pour the sauce over the fish and garnish with the red chili, coriander, pine nuts, and almonds. Serve warm.

Jordanian Spicy Fish

Preparation time: 10 minutes
Cook time: 28 minutes
Nutrition facts (per serving): 428 Cal (18g fat, 26g protein, 1g fiber)

Have you tried the Jordanian spicy fish before? Well, now you can enjoy this unique and flavorsome combination by cooking this recipe at home.

Ingredients (2 servings)
1 whole red snapper, cleaned
1 teaspoon salt
½ teaspoon black pepper, ground
2 teaspoon harissa paste
½ teaspoon pepper, crushed
4 lemon slices

Tarator Sauce
¼ cup olive oil
½ sweet onion, diced
8 garlic cloves, chopped
1 green pepper, diced
1 jalapeño pepper, diced
1 serrano pepper, diced
2 medium tomatoes, diced
1 teaspoon allspice, ground
½ teaspoon coriander, ground
½ teaspoon cumin, ground

½ teaspoon Aleppo pepper, crushed
Salt and black pepper, to taste
½ teaspoon cayenne pepper, ground
1 cup tahini
Juice of 2 lemons
1 cup Greek yogurt, full fat optional
1 handful of fresh parsley, chopped
1 handful of fresh cilantro, chopped
¼ cup toasted pine nuts, for garnish

Preparation

At 400 degrees F, preheat your oven. Place the fish on a suitable baking sheet. Rub the fish with harissa and stuff with lemons. Drizzle chili, black pepper, and salt on top. Bake the fish for 20 minutes in the oven. Sauté the onion with oil in a skillet until soft. Stir in the green pepper, serrano, jalapeno, and garlic. Next, then sauté for 8 minutes. Stir in all the spices and mix well. Mix the tahini with the lemon and pour into the skillet. Mix well and pour this sauce over the fish. Garnish with herbs and nuts. Serve warm.

Baba Ganouj

Preparation time: 15 minutes
Cook time: 20 minutes
Nutrition facts (per serving): 212 Cal (9g fat, 17g protein, 0.5g fiber)

The famous baba Ganouj recipe is here to make your Jordanian cuisine extra special. Make it with roasted eggplant slices for the best taste.

Ingredients (6 servings)
1 big eggplant, peeled and sliced
1 medium tomato, chopped
½ cup packed parsley, chopped
2 or 3 tablespoons pomegranate concentrate
⅓ cup pomegranate seeds
2 cloves mashed garlic
A dash of cumin
2 tablespoons olive oil
Salt and black pepper, to taste

Preparation
Brush the eggplant slices with oil in a baking pan lined with aluminum foil. Roast the slices for 20 minutes at 350 degrees F until soft. Cut the eggplants into chunks. Blend the eggplant in a blender. Add the parsley, garlic, spices, pomegranate concentrate, and salt. Next, blend for 1 minute. Stir in the tomato, pomegranate seeds, and olive oil. Serve.

Okra Stew

Preparation time: 10 minutes
Cook time: 1 hour 35 minutes
Nutrition facts (per serving): 270 Cal (12g fat, 24g protein, 6 g fiber)

This Okra stew has unique flavors due to its Bharat seasoning. Keep this seasoning ready in your kitchen to enjoy this mix whenever you want.

Ingredients (6 servings)
1-lb. small okra
1-lb. stew beef, chopped
28 oz. diced tomato
2 oz. tomato paste
1 cup beef broth
1 head garlic, peeled and chopped
3 tablespoons lemon juice
¼ cup and 2 tablespoons canola oil
1 tablespoon lemon juice
½ teaspoon Bharat
Salt and black pepper, to taste

Preparation
Sauté the okra with ¼ oil in a cooking pan over medium-high heat for 5 minutes and then transfer to a plate. Stir in the garlic and sauté until golden brown. Stir in the meat, salt, and black pepper. Then sauté until brown. Return the okra to the cooking pan and all the remaining ingredients. Cover and cook on a simmer for 1 ½ hour. Serve warm.

Perch Fillets with Tahini Sauce

Preparation time: 10 minutes
Cook time: 15 minutes
Nutrition facts (per serving): 416 Cal (28g fat, 17g protein, 1g fiber)

Let's make some perch fillets with tahini sauce with these simple ingredients. Mix them together and then cook to have a great combination of flavors.

Ingredients (4 servings)
4 ocean perch fillets
Lemon wedges, to serve

Tahini Sauce
1 small garlic clove, crushed
1 ½ tablespoon tahini
1 ½ tablespoon yogurt
1 lemon, juiced
1 ½ tablespoons water

Topping
5 garlic cloves, chopped
1 small red chili, deseeded, chopped
½ cup walnuts, chopped
⅓ cup pine nuts, chopped
½ cup coriander, chopped
2 green onions, chopped
1 teaspoon ground cumin
1 lemon, juiced
1 ½ tablespoon olive oil

Preparation

At 400 degrees F, preheat your oven. Layer a baking dish with a cooking spray. Mix all the sauce ingredients in a bowl. Mix the cumin and all the topping ingredients in a bowl. Place the fish in the prepared baking dish, add the toppings on top, and bake for 15 minutes. Pour the tahini sauce on top and serve.

Jordanian Spiced Rice and Fish

Preparation time: 10 minutes
Cook time: 41 minutes
Nutrition facts (per serving): 326 Cal (17g fat, 23g protein, 2g fiber)

This Jordanian spiced rice and fish entrée will melt your heart away with its epic flavors. The fish fillets are cooked and served with potatoes, pine nuts, and tahini sauce to make it taste even better and nutritious.

Ingredients (4 servings)

1 ⅔ lbs. Agria potatoes, chopped
3 tablespoons olive oil
2 red capsicums, cored, deseeded and chopped
1 teaspoon ground coriander
2 garlic clove, crushed
½ cup coriander, chopped
½ teaspoon chili flakes
Zest from 1 lemon
1 lb. firm white fish fillets
2 tablespoons toasted pine nuts
Lemon wedges, to serve

Tahini yoghurt sauce

¼ cup natural yogurt
1 small garlic clove, crushed
2 teaspoons tahini
Juice from ½ lemon

Preparation

At 400 degrees F, preheat your oven. Layer a baking sheet with wax paper. Toss the potato with 2 tablespoons olive oil and 1 pinch of salt in the baking sheet and roast for 20 minutes. Stir in the garlic, coriander, and capsicum and then roast for 15 minutes. Add the chili, zest, and coriander. Blend all the tahini ingredients in a blender. Set a suitable pan, greased with cooking oil and sear the fish for 3 minutes per side. Serve the fish with potatoes and tahini sauce. Garnish with lemon wedges. Serve warm.

Jordanian-Style Snapper

Preparation time: 10 minutes
Cook time: 25 minutes
Nutrition facts (per serving): 379 Cal (18g fat, 31g protein, 6g fiber)

This Jordanian style snapper has unique flavors due to its rich blend of onions and silver beets. Serve warm with your favorite bread on the side.

Ingredients (4 servings)
2 onions, sliced into rings
1 onion, chopped
4 oz. olive oil
1 garlic clove, crushed
6 silver beet leaves, leaves torn
1 ½ teaspoon sumac
4 baby snapper fillets, pin-boned
Coriander, chopped
Currants and toasted pine nuts

Tahini dressing
2 tablespoons tahini
Juice of 1 lemon
2 tablespoons olive oil
1 garlic clove, crushed

Preparation
Sauté the onion rings with 2 ½ tablespoons of oil in a cooking pot for 10 minutes and transfer to a plate. Sauté the onion and the garlic with 1

tablespoon olive oil in a frying pan for 4 minutes. Stir in the silver beet stalks and cook for 3 minutes. Stir in the beet leaves and cook for 2 minutes. Remove the mixture from the heat. Stir in ½ teaspoon sumac and mix well. Prepare the tahini sauce by blending all the ingredients. Add oil to a suitable frying pan and sear the snappers in the oil for 3 minutes per side. Serve the fish with the silver beets and caramelized onions on top. Enjoy the herb salad, currants, pine nuts, sumac, and tahini dressing. Serve.

Samak Mashwi

Preparation time: 15 minutes
Cook time: 25 minutes
Nutrition facts (per serving): 393 Cal (3g fat, 14g protein, 7g fiber)

If you haven't tried the famous Samak Mashwi loaded with two sauces, then here comes a simple and easy to cook recipe that you can recreate at home in no time with minimum efforts.

Ingredients (4 servings)
2 large fish
1 lemon, sliced
Rock Salt

The First Sauce
2 teaspoons cumin powder
2 teaspoons coriander powder
1 teaspoon chilli powder
1 teaspoon paprika
½ teaspoon turmeric powder
½ dried lemon, in powdered form
1 teaspoon white vinegar
Juice of 1 ½ lemons

The Second Sauce
1 cup onions, chopped
1 red capsicum, chopped
4 garlic cloves, chopped

2 cups tomato, chopped
5 tablespoons of olive oil
1 ½ teaspoon salt

Preparation

Mix all the ingredients for sauce 1 in a bowl. Sauté the tomatoes, garlic, and capsicum with oil in a skillet until soft. Transfer the mixture to a bowl. Place a foil sheet on a grill grate and set the fish on the sheet. Mix the remaining sauce in a bowl and add the mixture to the fish filling. Rub the prepared marinade over the fish and grill for 10 minutes. Flip and cook for another 10 minutes. Serve warm.

Jordanian Potato Kibbe

Preparation time: 15 minutes
Cook time: 80 minutes
Nutrition facts (per serving): 319 Cal (14g fat, 28g protein, 7g fiber)

Jordanian potato kibbe made from chickpeas, bulgur, and potatoes is one option to go for. Plus, if you have the chickpeas and boiled potatoes ready in your refrigerator, you can make it in no time.

Ingredients (8 servings)
2 cups of bulgur
2 cups dry chickpeas
3 medium-sized potatoes, boiled, mashed
2 cups flour
½ bunch parsley, chopped
½ bunch mint, chopped
½ bunch green onions, chopped
1 medium-sized white onion, chopped
1 teaspoon of cayenne pepper
½ teaspoon Jordanian 7-spices
⅔ teaspoon of salt
2 cups of olive oil

Preparation
Rinse and drain the chickpeas. Add the chickpeas and water to a cooking pot and cook until soft, then drain. Boil the potatoes in another pot with water for 20 minutes, then drain. Peel these potatoes and mash them in a mixing bowl. Soak the bulgur in water in a bowl for 30

minutes. Mix the flour with 7 spices, salt, cayenne pepper, mashed potatoes, and chickpeas and then mix well. Grease a glass baking pan with olive oil. Spread the prepared dough into ½ inch thick block. Cut the dough into squares and place them in the prepared pan. Bake them for 60 minutes at 400 degrees F. Flip the squares once cooked halfway through. Serve.

Jordanian Moussaka

Preparation time: 5 minutes
Cook time: 60 minutes
Nutrition facts (per serving): 376 Cal (14g fat, 22g protein, 18g fiber)

This Jordanian eggplant Moussaka recipe will make your day with its delightful taste. Serve warm with your favorite bread.

Ingredients (4 servings)

2 eggplants, peeled and diced
2 tomatoes, chopped
3 small onions, chopped
5 garlic cloves, chopped
1 can chickpeas
1 teaspoon salt
½ teaspoon cinnamon
¼ teaspoon cumin
¼ teaspoon chili powder
2 tablespoons olive oil
Water, as needed
1 teaspoon salt
½ cup olive oil

Preparation

At 425 degrees F, preheat your oven. Toss the eggplants with salt and oil on a suitable baking sheet and bake for 30 minutes. Broil the eggplant for 5 minutes. Sauté the onions with oil in a skillet for 5 minutes. Stir in the chickpeas, spice, and garlic. Then cook for 5 minutes. Stir in the tomatoes and cook for 10 minutes. Add the eggplants, cover, and cook for 5 minutes. Serve warm.

Jordanian Roasted Vegetables with Lentils

Preparation time: 15 minutes
Cook time: 75 minutes
Nutrition facts (per serving): 277 Cal (24g fat, 10g protein, 3g fiber)

If you want some new and exotic flavors in your meals, then this Jordanian roasted vegetables with lentils recipe is best to bring that variety to the menu.

Ingredients (6 servings)
Spice mix
1 teaspoon sweet paprika
1 teaspoon cumin
1 teaspoon ground coriander
1 teaspoon cardamom
½ teaspoon cinnamon
½ teaspoon nutmeg

Salad
¾ cup uncooked beluga lentils
3 tablespoons olive oil
1 medium sweet potato, peel and cut in short wedges
1 sweet red pepper, sliced
2 carrots, peeled and sliced
3 small red onion, cut into wedges
Salt and black pepper, to taste
Fresh parsley, to garnish
½ cup walnuts, toasted

Yogurt Sauce

½ cup Greek yogurt

4 tablespoons olive oil

Zest of ½ organic lemon

4 tablespoons lemon juice

1 tablespoon flat-leaf parsley, chopped

Preparation

At 400 degrees F, preheat your oven. Layer a baking sheet with parchment paper. Mix all the spice ingredients in a bowl. Cook the lentils as per the package's instruction in 3 times more water for 30 minutes and then drain. Toss the veggies with the spice mix, 2 tablespoons of olive oil on a suitable baking sheet, and bake for 30 minutes. Toss the veggies after 15 minutes. Mix all the yogurt sauce ingredients in a bowl. Add the lentils to the veggies and pour the sauce on top. Garnish with walnuts and parsley. Serve.

Mint Rice

Preparation time: 15 minutes
Cook time: 17 minutes
Nutrition facts (per serving): 341 Cal (11g fat, 4g protein, 5g fiber)

This mint rice is loved by all, young and adult. It's simple and quick to make and can be served with all stews, soups and curries.

Ingredients (4 servings)
4 ½ cups vegetable stock
2 cups basmati rice
¼ cup olive oil
1 tablespoon ground turmeric
2 teaspoons ground ginger
1 teaspoon salt

Fried Mint Leaves
1 bunch mint leaves
1 tablespoon coconut oil

Preparation
Add the rice, vegetable stock, olive oil, turmeric, and the rest of the ingredients in a saucepan. Cook for 15 minutes on a simmer until the rice is soft. Fry the mint leaves with the coconut oil in a skillet for 2 minutes. Garnish the rice with the fried mint. Serve.

Red Bulgur Pilaf

Preparation time: 15 minutes
Cook time: 37 minutes
Nutrition facts (per serving): 216 Cal (7g fat, 24g protein, 12g fiber)

The red Bulgur pilaf is famous for its unique taste and aroma, and now you can bring those exotic flavors home by using this recipe.

Ingredients (4 servings)
1 lb. (500 g) medium bulgur

2 lbs. (1 kg) tomatoes, chopped
2 green peppers
1 medium onion
½ ground lamb
2 tablespoons ghee
Salt and black pepper, to taste

Preparation
Dip all the tomatoes in boiling water for 1 minute and then remove. Peel these tomatoes and dice unto chunks. Sauté the onion with ghee in a skillet until soft. Stir in the green peppers and sauté for 1 minute. Stir in the ground meat and fry until brown. Add the tomatoes and cook on a simmer for 15 minutes. Add the black pepper and salt to adjust the seasoning. Stir in the bulgur and cook for 20 minutes on low heat. Serve warm.

Jordanian Chickpea Stew

Preparation time: 10 minutes
Cook time: 22 minutes
Nutrition facts (per serving): 344 Cal (41g fat, 34g protein, 3g fiber)

This Jordanian chickpea stew with tomato paste sauce will leave you drooling and craving for more. Try serving it with warm tortillas.

Ingredients (4 servings)
30 oz. can of chickpeas
5 garlic cloves
1 tablespoon cumin
3 teaspoons za'atar
2 bay leaves
1 teaspoon red pepper flakes
1 teaspoon paprika
2 tablespoons tomato paste
1 roasted bell pepper, chopped
2 teaspoon olive oil
Salt, to taste
2 tablespoons parsley, chopped

Preparation
Blend the cumin with garlic in a blender. Sauté this mixture with oil in a saucepan until golden brown. Stir in the tomato paste, paprika, and red pepper flakes. Sauté for 2 minutes. Stir in the chickpeas, zaatar, bay leaves, roasted red pepper, and 4 cups water. Cook for 15 minutes, add parsley, and then salt. Serve warm.

Jordanian Tofu Shish with Harissa Sauce

Preparation time: 15 minutes
Cook time: 40 minutes
Nutrition facts (per serving): 400 Cal (11g fat, 5g protein, 4g fiber)

The Jordanian tofu shish with Harissa Sauce will melt your heart with its great taste and texture. Serve warm with white rice.

Ingredients (20 servings)
Tofu Shish
1 block tofu drained and pressed, diced
4 tablespoons soy yogurt
1 tablespoon tomato puree
2 tablespoons lemon juice
3 garlic cloves, crushed
½ teaspoon turmeric
½ teaspoon ground cumin
½ teaspoon black pepper
½ teaspoon sea salt
1 teaspoon cayenne pepper
1 teaspoon ground paprika
1 red onion, chopped
1 red pepper, chopped
1 yellow pepper, chopped
2 tablespoons olive oil

Harissa Sauce

4 tablespoons plain soy yogurt
1 garlic clove, crushed
1 tablespoon harissa paste
½ tablespoon lemon juice
Salt and black pepper, to taste

Preparation

Blend the yogurt with garlic, lemon juice, and tomato puree in a bowl. Stir in the paprika, cayenne pepper, salt, black pepper, cumin, and turmeric. Mix well, toss in the tofu, cover, and refrigerate for 30 minutes. Blend all the harissa ingredients in a blender until smooth. Grease a griddle pan with 1 tablespoon olive oil and heat over medium-high heat. Add the red onion, yellow and red pepper, and then cook for 5 minutes per side. Transfer the veggies to a plate. Grill the tofu in the same pan with olive oil for 5 minutes per side. Add the tofu to the veggies and garnish with harissa dressing. Serve.

Jordanian Rice and Lentils

Preparation time: 10 minutes
Cook time: 51 minutes
Nutrition facts (per serving): 286 Cal (13g fat, 19g protein, 2g fiber)

Let's have a rich and delicious combination of rice and lentils. Cook it at home and serve warm with garlic yogurt on top.

Ingredients (8 servings)
2 cups sunflower oil
4 onions, sliced
1 handful plain flour
7 oz. green lentils
3 tablespoons olive oil
2 tablespoons cumin seeds
2 tablespoons coriander seeds
½ teaspoon ground turmeric
1½ teaspoon ground cinnamon
9 oz. basmati rice
1 pinch caster sugar
1 bunch fresh coriander

Garlic Yogurt
1 cup Greek yogurt
3 spring onions, sliced
1 garlic clove, crushed
2 tablespoons olive oil

Preparation

Sauté the onions with flour and oil in a frying pan for 4 minutes. Transfer the onions to a plate lined with parchment paper. Boil the lentils in a cooking pot as per the package's instructions. Drain and mix the lentils with the olive oil. Sauté the cumin and coriander seeds with 2 tablespoons of oil in a frying pan for 1 minute. Stir in the cinnamon and the turmeric and cook for 1 minute. Add the sugar, rice, spices, black pepper, salt, water, and lentils. Cook for 15 minutes on a simmer. Mix all the garlic yogurt ingredients in a bowl. Serve the rice with fried onions and yogurt on top. Garnish with coriander. Enjoy.

Jordanian Green Beans

Preparation time: 10 minutes
Cook time: 15 minutes
Nutrition facts (per serving): 178 Cal (10g fat, 4g protein, 2g fiber)

If you can't think of anything delicious and savory to serve, then try these Jordanian green beans because of their great taste and texture to serve at the table.

Ingredients (4 servings)
1 cup onions yellow, chopped
3 garlic cloves
8 oz. tomatoes
1 lb. French green beans
½ teaspoon sea salt
¼ teaspoon white pepper
¼ teaspoon black pepper
⅛ teaspoon cinnamon

Preparation
Sauté the onions with oil in a skillet for 1 minute. Stir in the garlic and sauté for 6 minutes. Stir in the tomatoes and the spices and sauté for 5 minutes. Stir in the beans and then cook for 3 minutes. Serve warm.

Grilled Snapper with Bulgar Salad

Preparation time: 15 minutes
Cook time: 20 minutes
Nutrition facts (per serving): 225 Cal (4g fat, 14g protein, 1g fiber)

This grilled snapper with bulgur salad is one of the Jordanian specialties, and everyone must try this interesting combination of bulgur with rocket and tomatoes.

Ingredients (8 servings)

3 garlic cloves, peeled
1 tablespoon ground cumin
2 teaspoons sweet paprika
2 tablespoons white vinegar
⅓ cup olive oil
2 ½ lbs. snapper, cleaned, scored
1½ cups coarse bulgur
2 bunches arugula or rocket, trimmed, chopped
2 tomatoes, chopped
1 small red onion, chopped
1 cup parsley leaves
2 small lemons, juiced
2 teaspoons sumac

Preparation

Crush the garlic with 1 teaspoon salt, paprika, and cumin in a mortar using a pestle. Stir in 2 tablespoons of oil and vinegar and then mix well. Rub this mixture over the snapper, cover, and refrigerate for 30 minutes. Soak the bulgur in boiling water for 20 minutes, then drain, and fluff. Set a grill over medium heat and grill for the marinated fish for 10 minutes per side. Mix the rest of the ingredients in a bowl. Serve the fish with salad and enjoy.

Baked Fish with Garlic and Lemon

Preparation time: 15 minutes
Cook time: 35 minutes
Nutrition facts (per serving): 265 Cal (13g fat, 13g protein, 0.2g fiber)

You can't really imagine a Jordanian menu with having this baked fish meal in it. Now you can serve with some sautéed green beans and bacon.

Ingredients (2 servings)
2 (4 lbs.) whole red snapper fish
2 lemons, juiced
1 lemon, cut into 8 pieces
7 tablespoons olive oil
2 garlic heads, peeled and crushed
1 teaspoon of salt

Preparation
Cut ½ inch deep cuts on top of the fish and drizzle some salt on top. Blend the garlic with ½ teaspoon of salt and 7 tablespoons olive oil blender. Place the fish on an aluminum foil and drizzle garlic sauce over the fish and add lemon chunks on top. Wrap the fish and bake for 35 minutes in the oven at 400 degrees F. Serve warm.

Desserts

Jordanian Baklava

Preparation time: 10 minutes
Cook time: 50 minutes
Nutrition facts (per serving): 393 Cal (18g g fat, 9g protein, 3g fiber)

Jordanian Baklava is another layered dessert that has phyllo sheets layered with butter, sugar, and walnuts filling. These layers are topped with sugar syrup.

Ingredients (8 servings)
1 lb. (500 g) frozen phyllo, thawed
1 lb. (500 g) unsalted butter, melted
1 lb. (500 g) walnuts, ground
1 ½ cups sugar
Dash cinnamon
1 teaspoon rosewater

Syrup
2 cups of sugar
2 cups of water
1 teaspoon lemon juice

Preparation
Mix the sugar, rosewater, cinnamon, and walnuts in a bowl. Grease an 8x8 inch pan with cooking oil and place two phyllo sheets at its bottom. Brush them with butter and drizzle ¼ of the walnut mixture. Add another two sheets of phyllo on top, brush them with butter, and drizzle ¼ walnut mixture. Repeat the layers with the phyllo sheet on top. Slice

the layers into 24 squares. Bake the layers for 45 minutes in the oven at 325 degrees F until golden brown from top. Meanwhile, prepare the syrup by mixing sugar and water in a pan over low heat and cook until it thickens. Remove its pan from the heat and allow it to cool. Stir in the lemon juice and then mix well. Pour the syrup on top of the baked baklava and allow it to absorb the syrup. Enjoy!

Qatayef

Preparation time: 15 minutes
Cook time: 25 minutes
Nutrition facts (per serving): 347 Cal (15g fat, 7g protein, 5g fiber)

A dessert that has no parallel, the Qatayef is made with semolina, flour dough, and a creamy ricotta filling.

Ingredients (8 servings)
Dough
1¼ cup flour
⅓ cup extra-fine semolina
1½ cup whole milk
1 teaspoon active dry yeast
1 teaspoon baking powder
2 tablespoons caster sugar

Cream
1 cup ricotta
½ cup heavy cream
¾ cup whole milk
2 teaspoons semolina
3 tablespoons orange blossom water
½ cup pistachios, crushed

Syrup
1 cup caster sugar
1½ cup of water
3 tablespoons orange blossom water
A few drops lemon juice

Preparation

Mix the yeast with half of the milk in a bowl and leave for 5 minutes. Mix the flour with semolina, baking powder, and caster sugar in a mixing bowl. Stir in the yeast mixture and the remaining milk and then mix well until it makes smooth dough. Cover this qatayef dough with a kitchen towel and leave for 1 hour. Place a non-stick skillet over medium heat. Take 4 tablespoons of this dough and spread it into a thin layer and cook this thin crepe for 2-3 minutes per side. Repeat the same with the remaining dough. Mix the milk, semolina, and cream in a saucepan and stir cook until it thickens. Cover the cream with plastic wrap and refrigerate until cooled. Add the ricotta or the mascarpone to the cream and mix well. Prepare the syrup by mixing the sugar, orange blossom water, and water in a saucepan and cook this mixture until it thickens. Stir in the lemon juice and mix well. Then allow it to cool. Place the pancakes on the working surface, top them with the cream mixture, roll them, and top the rolls with sugar syrup. Enjoy.

Warbat

Preparation time: 15 minutes
Cook time: 33 minutes
Nutrition facts (per serving): 360 Cal (14g fat, 8g protein, 1g fiber)

This Jordanian warbat dessert makes an easy way to enjoy a fancy dessert, and this recipe will let you bake a delicious cake in no time.

Ingredients (8 servings)
1 (16 oz) pack phyllo dough
¾ cup vegetable shortening melted
¾ cup unsalted butter, melted
¼ cup ground pistachios

Ashta Filling
3 cups whole milk
1 cup heavy cream
⅔ cup corn starch
⅓ cup sugar
1 tablespoon rose water
1 ½ tablespoon orange blossom water

Sugar Syrup
2 cups of sugar
1 cup of water
1 tablespoon orange blossom water
½ tablespoon rose water
1 teaspoon lemon juice

Preparation

For the filling, mix all the ingredients in a saucepan. Boil this mixture, reduce its heat, and cook on low heat until it thickens. Remove it from the heat and spread it in a Pyrex dish. Cover it with plastic wrap and refrigerate for 30 minutes. Meanwhile, prepare the syrup and mix all its ingredients in a saucepan. Cook for 2 minutes on a simmer, then allow it to cool. Melt butter and shortening in a glass bowl by heating in the microwave for 1 minute. Spread a phyllo sheet on the working surface and brush the top with butter mixture. Repeat the phyllo and butter layers to stack 15 sheets on top of another. Cut these sheets into squares. Add a teaspoon of filling at the center of each square and fold it in half. Place the pastries on a suitable baking sheet lined with wax paper. Bake for 30 minutes in the oven. Allow the pastries to cool and pour the syrup over them. Serve.

Mahalebia

Preparation time: 10 minutes
Cook time: 6 minutes
Nutrition facts (per serving): 319 Cal (10g fat, 5g protein, 4g fiber)

Count on this Jordanian Mahalebia dessert to make your dessert menu extra special and surprise your loved one with the ultimate flavors.

Ingredients (4 servings)
2 cups of milk
4 tablespoons of cornstarch
2 tablespoons of sugar
½ teaspoon of rosewater
2 tablespoons of crushed pistachios

Preparation
Mix the milk with sugar and cornstarch in a saucepan and cook for 5 minutes on medium heat until it thickens. Stir in the rosewater and cook for 1 minute. Divide the dessert in the serving bowls and garnish with pistachios. Serve.

Jordanian Semolina Pudding

Preparation time: 5 minutes
Cook time: 15 minutes
Nutrition facts (per serving): 353 Cal (18g fat, 7g protein, 4g fiber)

Simple and easy to make, this Jordanian Semolina Pudding is a must to try on this menu. Jordanian pudding dessert is a delight to add to your dessert menu when covered with raspberry sauce.

Ingredients (6 servings)
2 cups of milk
1 teaspoon rose water
1 cup table cream
1 cup powdered milk
1 cup and half water
1 ½ tablespoon corn starch
1 teaspoon sugar
1 teaspoon rose water
Crushed pistachio, for garnish

Preparation
Mix the milk with semolina in a medium pot and cook for 15 minutes until the mixture thickens. Divide the dessert into small cups, allow it to cool, and refrigerate for 2 hours. Top the dessert with table cream and garnish with pistachios. Refrigerate for 24 hours and serve.

Jordanian Semolina Cake Halva

Preparation time: 15 minutes
Cook time: 10 minutes
Nutrition facts (per serving): 292 Cal (9g fat, 11g protein, 4g fiber)

The Jordanian semolina halva is not only delicious, but it also makes a healthy and loaded dessert. You can serve this dessert with hot beverages.

Ingredients (6 servings)
Namoura
5 cups semolina
1 cup fine semolina
2 cups butter or ghee, melted
2 cups of sugar
2 ½ cups plain yogurt
2 teaspoons baking powder
1 ½ teaspoon orange blossom water
1 ½ teaspoon rose water
1 cup almonds, blanched
3 tablespoons tahini

Sugar Syrup
3 cups of sugar
3 cups of water
1 teaspoon lemon juice
1 teaspoon orange blossom water
1 teaspoon rose water

Preparation

Mix all the ingredients for namoura in a bowl. Spread the tahini in a 15 inch round pan. Add the namoura batter into the pan and spread evenly. Leave this mixture for 6 hours. Cut the mixture into diamond-shaped pieces. Garnish with nuts. Mix the sugar with water, lemon juice, blossom water, and rose water in a saucepan and cook until the syrup thickens. Pour this syrup over the namoura and allow it to cool. Serve.

Halawa

Preparation time: 15 minutes
Cook time: 45 minutes
Nutrition facts (per serving): 321 Cal (21g fat, 4g protein, 1.4g fiber)

These sugary halawet el jibn rolls with cheese filling are the most flavorsome dessert recipe that you can try for your Jordanian dessert menu.

Ingredients (6 servings)
Sugar syrup
2 cups caster sugar
1 cup of water
½ teaspoon lemon juice
¾ teaspoon orange blossom water
¾ teaspoon rose water

Cheese rolls
1½ cup of water
¾ cup caster sugar
1 cup fine semolina
8-oz. akkawi and majdoola cheese
1 tablespoon rose water
1 tablespoon orange blossom water
14-oz. ashta (Jordanian cream)
Crushed pistachios
Rose petals jam

Preparation

Mix the water with caster sugar and lemon juice in a saucepan over medium-high heat. Boil this lemon mixture and cook for 12 minutes on a low simmer until it thickens. Allow the syrup to cool. Add rosewater and orange blossom water. Mix the water with sugar in another saucepan. Boil it, add semolina, and then cook for 30 seconds until it thickens. Reduce its heat, add rose water and cheese, and then cook until the cheese is melted. Allow it to cool and divide this dough into four equal portions. Spread each portion into a 9x13 inches sheet using a rolling pin onto parchment paper squares. Add ashta to a piping bag and pipe on top of each dough sheet. Roll the semolina dough by rolling the parchment paper underneath them. Refrigerate these rolls for 30 minutes. Evenly, pour the sugar syrup on top of the rolls and garnish with pistachios and petal jams.

Sweet Dumplings

Preparation time: 10 minutes
Cook time: 10 minutes
Nutrition facts (per serving): 186 Cal (12g fat, 2.4g protein, 2.5g fiber)

Without these sweet dumplings, it seems like the Jordanian dessert menu is incomplete. Try them with different variations of toppings.

Ingredients (12 servings)
2 cups flour
2 cups warm water
2 teaspoons instant yeast
2 teaspoons sugar
1 tablespoon corn starch
Oil, for frying

Sugar Syrup
1 cup of sugar
1 cup of water
1 teaspoon lemon juice
1 teaspoon rose water

Preparation
Mix the flour, cornstarch, warm water, yeast, and sugar in a bowl to make a soft dough. Cover this dough with plastic wrap and leave for 1 hour. Make golf-ball sized balls from this mixture and roll them in your oiled hands. Pour cooking oil into a deep frying pan and heat it to 350

degrees F. Deep fry the balls until golden brown. Transfer the balls to a colander and allow them to cool. Prepare the syrup by mixing sugar and water in a saucepan and cook until it thickens. Allow it to cool and then add rosewater and lemon juice. Dip the balls in the syrup for few seconds and then serve.

Sesame Cookies

Preparation time: 10 minutes
Cook time: 30 minutes
Nutrition facts (per serving): 374 Cal (14g fat, 7g protein, 2g fiber)

These Jordan baked sesame cookies are worth the try as they taste so unique and exotic. This dessert is definitely a must to have on the Jordanian menu.

Ingredients (6 servings)

Honey Syrup
¼ cup honey
¼ cup water

Cookies
7 oz. (200 g) white sesame seeds
6 oz. (175 g) unsalted butter
5 oz. (150 g) granulated sugar
1 teaspoon baking powder
1 teaspoon ground mahlab
11 oz. (312 g) all-purpose flour
1 teaspoon (2 ½ g) active dry yeast
3 oz. skimmed milk
2 tablespoons chopped or slivered raw pistachio

Preparation

Mix the honey with the water in a saucepan and cook a simmer for 3 minutes and then allow it to cool. Meanwhile, in a skillet, toast sesame seeds for 5 minutes and then allow them to cool. Beat the butter with the sugar in a bowl. Stir in the baking powder, mahlab, yeast, flour, and milk and then mix well until it makes a smooth dough. Cover this dough with plastic wrap and leave it for 15 minutes, at 325 degrees F, and layer two baking sheets with parchment paper. Make golf-ball sized balls from this dough and flatten the balls into cookies. Dip each cookie in honey syrup and coat them with sesame seeds and pistachios. Place them on a suitable baking sheet and bake them for 30 minutes. Serve.

Jordanian Bread Pudding

Preparation time: 10 minutes
Cook time: 25 minutes
Nutrition facts (per serving): 391 Cal (51g fat, 13g protein, 2g fiber)

Have you ever tried the Jordanian bread pudding? If not, then here comes a recipe that will help you cook the finest pudding in no time.

Ingredients (8 servings)
8 bread slices

Simple Syrup
⅓ cup sugar
½ cup water
½ tablespoon rosewater

Cream Base
1 ½ cup milk
⅔ cup cream
2 ½ tablespoons corn flour
4 tablespoons sugar
½ tablespoon rose water
½ tablespoon orange blossom water
Chopped pistachios, for garnishing

Preparation
Spread the bread cubes in an 8-inch baking dish. Bake them for 15 minutes at 400 degrees F. Mix the water with the sugar in a cooking pan

and cook until caramelized. Remove the syrup from the heat and add rose water. Allow it to cool. Pour this syrup over the baked bread. Mix milk with sugar and cream in a saucepan. Mix the corn flour with 2 tablespoons of water and pour into the milk. Cook until the mixture thickens. Allow the mixture to cool. Stir in the orange blossom water and the rosewater. Pour this pudding over the bread, cover with a cling film, and allow it to cool. Refrigerate for 1 hour, slice, and serve.

Maamoul

Preparation time: 15 minutes
Cook time: 20 minutes
Nutrition facts (per serving): 149 Cal (10g fat, 4g protein, 0g fiber)

The maamoul is a Jordan-style special cookie that you need to add to your dessert menu. You serve these cookies with chocolate dips as well.

Ingredients (10 servings)
Dough
3 ¼ cups durum wheat flour
2 ¼ cups all-purpose flour
1 cup softened butter
¾ cup icing sugar
1 ½ teaspoon baking powder
¼ cup milk
¼ cup orange blossom water

Filling
8 oz. date paste
3 tablespoons toasted walnuts, crushed
5 tablespoons toasted pistachios, crushed
3 tablespoons toasted almonds, crushed

Preparation
Prepare the filling by mixing date paste, walnuts, pistachios, and almonds in a bowl. To prepare the dough, mix the semolina with icing sugar, flour, baking powder, and butter in a mixing bowl. Stir in the

milk and the orange blossom water and then mix until it makes a smooth dough. Cover the dough with plastic wrap and leave for 15 minutes. Make ½ oz. weighing balls out of this dough and roll them in the nuts' mixture. Place the balls in the maamoul molds and press to get the desired shape. Transfer the maamoul balls to a baking sheet lined with a parchment sheet and bake them for 20 minutes. Garnish with the icing sugar and serve.

Jordanian Rice Pudding

Preparation time: 15 minutes
Cook time: 40 minutes
Nutrition facts (per serving): 396 Cal (23g fat, 8g protein, 0g fiber)

If you haven't tried the delicious Jordanian rice pudding before, then here comes a simple and easy cook this recipe that you can recreate at home in no time with minimum efforts.

Ingredients (6 servings)
5 oz. pudding rice
1 cup double cream
1 cup full-fat milk
2 tablespoons golden caster sugar
1 vanilla pod, split
16 dried apricots
1 cinnamon stick
½ unwaxed lemon
2 teaspoons rosewater
2 teaspoons orange blossom water
1 ¾ oz. shelled pistachios, chopped
2 tablespoons food-grade rose petals

Preparation
Mix the rice with the milk, sugar, vanilla pod, and cream in a cooking pan and cook to a boil. Reduce its heat and cook for 25 minutes with occasional stirring. Boil the apricots with water, lemon, and a cinnamon stick and cook for 10 minutes on a simmer. Add orange blossom and

rosewater to the rice pudding and discard the vanilla pod. Divide this pudding into the serving bowls. Divide the apricots on top of the pudding. Garnish with pistachios and rose petals. Allow the pudding to cool and serve.

Sfouf Mini Cakes

Preparation time: 10 minutes
Cook time: 22 minutes
Nutrition facts (per serving): 274 Cal (3g fat, 11g protein, 3g fiber)

Have you tried the famous sfouf mini cakes? If you haven't, now is the time to cook these delicious cakes at home using simple and healthy ingredients.

Ingredients (6 servings)
1½ cups all-purpose flour
½ cup fine semolina
1⅓ cup white granulated sugar
¾ cup water
¾ cup olive oil
1 tablespoon turmeric
1½ teaspoon baking powder
1 tablespoon raw slivered almonds

Preparation
Grease a 12 cup liner with a cooking spray. At 375 degrees F, preheat your oven. Mix the flour with the baking powder, turmeric, sugar, and semolina in a bowl. Stir in the water and oil and mix evenly. Divide this mixture into the muffin tray. Drizzle almonds on top and bake for 22 minutes in the oven. Allow the cakes to cool and serve.

Kanafeh

Preparation time: 15 minutes
Cook time: 25 minutes
Nutrition facts (per serving): 242 Cal (14g fat, 12g protein, 1g fiber)

This angel hair kanafeh is another good serving that is famous in Jordan. It's prepared using the basic ingredients.

Ingredients (6 servings)
Kanafeh
8 oz. kadaïf angel hair
16 oz. akawi cheese
⅔ cup samneh clarified butter
3 oz. crushed pistachios
¼ teaspoon orange food coloring

Syrup
½ cup of water
1½ cup caster sugar
3 teaspoons rose water
Confectioners' sugar, for dusting

Preparation
Slice the akawi cheese into slices and soak them in water. At 350 degrees F, preheat your oven. Blend Kadar in a blender, then add melted butter, then mix well. Spread this mixture in a baking dish. Grate the cheese and spread over the kadaif. Next, bake for 25 minutes. Meanwhile, mix the sugar with water in a cooking pot on low heat and then stir in rose water. Pour this syrup on top of the baked kanafeh and drizzle with pistachios. Slice and serve.

Caramelized Dates

Preparation time: 15 minutes
Cook time: 10 minutes
Nutrition facts (per serving): 115 Cal (0.9g fat, 1g protein, 3g fiber)

Caramelized tamarind is one option to go for in the desserts. You can also keep them ready and stored and then use it as a spread or a dessert topping.

Ingredients (6 servings)
8 oz. dates, pitted and chopped
1 teaspoon ghee
1 teaspoon sugar

Preparation
Melt the ghee in a cooking pot, add the dates and then stir fry for 5-10 minutes until caramelized. Drizzle sugar on top and mix well. Serve.

Sesame Pistachio Cookies

Preparation time: 10 minutes
Cook time: 30 minutes
Nutrition facts (per serving): 374 Cal (14g fat, 7g protein, 2g fiber)

These Jordanian baked sesame cookies are worth the try as they taste so unique and exotic. This dessert is definitely a must to have on the Jordanian menu.

Ingredients (6 servings)
Honey Syrup
¼ cup honey
¼ cup water

Cookies
7 oz. (200 g) white sesame seeds
6 oz. (175 g) unsalted butter
5 oz. (150 g) granulated sugar
1 teaspoon baking powder
1 teaspoon ground mahlab
11 oz. (312 g) all-purpose flour
1 teaspoon (2 ½ g) active dry yeast
3 oz. skimmed milk
2 tablespoons chopped or slivered raw pistachio

Preparation
Mix the honey with water in a saucepan, cook a simmer for 3 minutes, and then allow it to cool. Meanwhile, in a skillet, toast the sesame seeds

for 5 minutes and then allow them to cool. Beat the butter with the sugar in a bowl. Stir in the baking powder, mahlab, yeast, flour, and milk then mix well until it makes a smooth dough. Cover this dough with plastic wrap and leave it for 15 minutes, at 325 degrees F, and layer two baking sheets with parchment paper. Make golf-ball sized balls from this dough and flatten the balls into cookies. Dip each cookie in honey syrup and coat them with sesame seeds and pistachios. Place them in a baking sheet and bake them for 30 minutes. Serve.

Drinks

Sahlab

Preparation time: 5 minutes
Cook time: 2 minutes
Nutrition facts (per serving): 222 Cal (14g fat, 7g protein, 0.8g fiber)

A creamy mix of milk, nuts, and sugar is all that you need to expand your Jordanian menu. Simple and easy to make, this recipe is a must to try.

Ingredients (6 servings)

4 cups (1 liter) whole milk
3 ½ tablespoons (¾ oz.) cornstarch
6 teaspoons granulated sugar
1 teaspoon pure vanilla extract
½ teaspoon ground cinnamon
1 tablespoon desiccated coconut
¼ cup chopped nuts, walnuts, or pistachios
2 tablespoons raisins optional

Preparation

Whisk the sugar, milk, vanilla, and cornstarch in a cooking pot and cook for 2 minutes. Pour into the serving glasses. Garnish with nuts, coconut, and cinnamon. Serve.

Qamar Ad-Din

Preparation time: 5 minutes
Nutrition facts (per serving): 156 Cal (0g fat, 0.7g protein, 1.4g fiber)

The Sharab Qamar Ad-din drink is all that you need to celebrate the holidays. Keep the drink ready in your refrigerator for quick serving.

Ingredients (2 servings)
9 oz. (250 g) sheet of dried apricot paste, cut into pieces
3 tablespoons sugar
2 cups (450 ml) water
2 ice cubes

Preparation
Add the water and the sugar to a jug and mix well until the sugar is dissolved. Add the apricot paste, soak, and refrigerate for 24 hours. Blend the apricot mixture for 2 minutes. Add 2 ice cubes and blend until crushed. Strain the drink and serve.

Tamar Hindi

Preparation time: 5 minutes

Nutrition facts (per serving): 63 Cal (0g fat, 3g protein, 1g fiber)

The tamarind drink is loved by all due to its refreshing taste. It's rich in energy and nutrients.

Ingredients (1 serving)
3 tablespoons tamarind date chutney
1 cup (250 ml) cold water
3 drops rose water

Preparation
Pour or add all the ingredients to a blender and blend for 60 seconds. Serve.

Shaneeneh

Preparation time: 5 minutes
Nutrition facts (per serving): 178 Cal (12g fat, 17g protein, 0.7g fiber)

Shaneeneh is a perfect sweet and savory drink made from yogurt and water. It has quite a calming effect on the mind and the body.

Ingredients (1 servings)
½ cup of yogurt cold
½ cup of water cold
¼ teaspoon salt
Fresh mint or dried
Crushed ice

Preparation
Pour or add all the ingredients to a blender and blend for 60 seconds. Serve.

Jallab

Preparation time: 5 minutes
Nutrition facts (per serving): 120 Cal (0g fat, 1g protein, 1g fiber)

Here's a special Jordanian Jallab drink that's made out of Jallab syrup, pine nuts, and golden raisins for a super refreshing treat.

Ingredients (1 serving)
3 tablespoons Jallab syrup
1 tablespoon golden raisins
1 tablespoon pine nuts
Crushed ice

Preparation
Blend the syrup with the raisins, nuts, and ice in a blender. Serve.

Cardamom Coffee

Preparation time: 10 minutes
Cook time: 5 minutes
Nutrition facts (per serving): 30 Cal (0g fat, 0g protein, 5g fiber)

The Jordanian cardamom coffee is great to serve on all special occasions and dinner, especially during the winter holidays.

Ingredients (2 servings)
8 oz. of water
5 teaspoons ground coffee
4 cardamom pods, grounded
2 dashes cinnamon
1 dash grated ginger
Sugar

Preparation
Mix the water, sugar, ginger, cardamom, cinnamon, and coffee in a saucepan and cook until it boils. Serve warm.

Jordanian Rose Drink

Preparation time: 5 minutes
Cook time: 5 minutes
Nutrition facts (per serving): 122 Cal (0g fat, 1g protein, 0 g fiber)

This refreshing Jordanian rose drink is always a delight to serve at parties. Now you can make it easily at home by using the following simple ingredients.

Ingredients (6 servings)
5 tablespoons brown sugar
Juice of 1 lemon
1 (750 ml) bottle red wine
2 cups orange juice
2 cups black tea
1 ½ teaspoon vanilla extract
1 lemon, sliced
1 orange, sliced
1 cinnamon stick
8 whole cloves
7 tablespoons marzipan
1 oz. semi-sweet chocolate
¾ cup rum

Preparation
Boil the sugar, water, and lemon juice in a saucepan for 5 minutes. Remove it from the heat and stir in the rest of the ingredients. Mix well and allow it to cool. Add ice and serve.

Jordanian Lemonade

Preparation time: 5 minutes
Nutrition facts (per serving): 161 Cal (0g fat, 3g protein, 1g fiber)

This Jordanian limonada drink is a great beverage to serve at any time. It delivers a unique blend of lemon juice and rose water.

Ingredients (1 serving)
½ cup lemon juice
2 lemon, zested
3 tablespoons sugar
1 teaspoon rose water
12 oz. lemon mineral water
Ice

Garnish
20 mint leaves

Preparation
Blend all the lemonade ingredients in a blender. Garnish with mint and serve with ice.

If you liked Jordanian recipes, discover to how cook DELICIOUS recipes from **Balkan** countries!

Within these pages, you'll learn 35 authentic recipes from a Balkan cook. These aren't ordinary recipes you'd find on the Internet, but recipes that were closely guarded by our Balkan mothers and passed down from generation to generation.

Main Dishes, Appetizers, and Desserts included!

If you want to learn how to make Croatian green peas stew, and 32 other authentic Balkan recipes, then start with our book!

Order at www.balkanfood.org/cook-books/ for only $2,99

Maybe Hungarian cuisine?

Order at www.balkanfood.org/cook-books/ for only $2,99

If you're a **Mediterranean** dieter who wants to know the secrets of the Mediterranean diet, dieting, and cooking, then you're about to discover how to master cooking meals on a Mediterranean diet right now!

In fact, if you want to know how to make Mediterranean food, then this new e-book - "The 30-minute Mediterranean diet" - gives you the answers to many important questions and challenges every Mediterranean dieter faces, including:

- How can I succeed with a Mediterranean diet?
- What kind of recipes can I make?
- What are the key principles to this type of diet?
- What are the suggested weekly menus for this diet?
- Are there any cheat items I can make?

... and more!

If you're serious about cooking meals on a Mediterranean diet and you really want to know how to make Mediterranean food, then you need to grab a copy of "The 30-minute Mediterranean diet" right now.

Prepare **111 recipes with several ingredients in less than 30 minutes**!

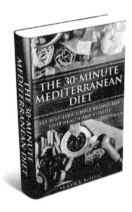

Order at www.balkanfood.org/cook-books/ for only $2,99

What could be better than a home-cooked meal? Maybe only a **Greek** homemade meal.

Do not get discouraged if you have no Greek roots or friends. Now you can make a Greek food feast in your kitchen.

This ultimate Greek cookbook offers you 111 best dishes of this cuisine! From more famous gyros to more exotic *Kota Kapama* this cookbook keeps it easy and affordable.

All the ingredients necessary are wholesome and widely accessible.
The author's picks are as flavorful as they are healthy. The dishes described in this cookbook are "what Greek mothers have made for decades."

Full of well-balanced and nutritious meals, this handy cookbook includes many vegan options. Discover a plethora of benefits of Mediterranean cuisine, and you may fall in love with cooking at home.

Inspired by a real food lover, this collection of delicious recipes will taste buds utterly satisfied.

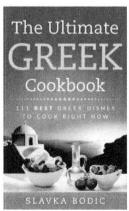

Order at www.balkanfood.org/cook-books/ for only $2,99

Maybe some Swedish meatballs ?

Order at www.balkanfood.org/cook-books/ for only $2,99

Maybe to try exotic **Syrian** cuisine?

From succulent *sarma*, soups, warm and cold salads to delectable desserts, the plethora of flavors will satisfy the most jaded foodie. Have a taste of a new culture with this **traditional Syrian cookbook**.

Order at www.balkanfood.org/cook-books/ for only $2,99

Maybe **Polish** cuisine?

Order at www.balkanfood.org/cook-books/ for only $2,99

Or **Peruvian?**

Order at www.balkanfood.org/cook-books/ for only $2,99

ONE LAST THING

If you enjoyed this book or found it useful, I'd be very grateful if you could find the time to post a short review on Amazon. Your support really does make a difference and I read all the reviews personally, so I can get your feedback and make this book even better.

Thanks again for your support!

Please send me your feedback at

www.balkanfood.org

Made in the USA
Coppell, TX
16 May 2023